THE FEMALE IN ARISTOTLE'S BIOLOGY

THE FEMALE IN ARISTOTLE'S BIOLOGY

REASON OR RATIONALIZATION

ROBERT MAYHEW

The University of Chicago Press
Chicago and London

Robert Mayhew is associate professor of philosophy at Seton
Hall University. He is the author of *Aristotle's Criticism of Plato's
"Republic."*

The University of Chicago Press, Chicago 60637
The University of Chicago Press, Ltd., London
© 2004 by The University of Chicago
All rights reserved. Published 2004
Printed in the United States of America

13 12 11 10 09 08 07 06 05 04   1 2 3 4 5

ISBN: 0-226-51200-2 (cloth)

Library of Congress Cataloging-in-Publication Data
  Mayhew, Robert
  The female in Aristotle's biology : reason or rationalization /
  Robert Mayhew.
    p. cm.
  Includes bibliographical references (p.   ) and index.
  ISBN 0-226-51200-2
  1. Misogyny.   2. Women.   3. Aristotle.   I. Title.
  HQ1233 .M359   2004
  305.4—dc22

                            2003019202

#NJG; 249

CONTENTS

Aristotle's writings on females are notorious. My aim is not to defend them but to defend Aristotle against the common charge that, in his biological writings, his conclusions about females are the result not of honest philosophy and science but of "ideology." I believe such an exploration of the relevant sections of his biological writings not only clears Aristotle of this charge but also enables us to better understand the nature of his views and how he may have come to hold them.

My intended audience is broad. This book should be of interest not only to scholars of Aristotle's philosophy and science but also to anyone interested in the history and philosophy of science generally, classical studies, and women studies. All Greek passages have been translated. For Aristotle's *Parts of Animals,* I have used James Lennox's translation in the Clarendon Aristotle Series (Oxford: Oxford University Press, 2001); for the *Generation of Animals,* I have used David Balme's Clarendon Aristotle translation of book 1 (Oxford: Oxford University Press, 1972) and Peck's Loeb Classical Library translation of books 2–5 (Cambridge, Mass.: Harvard University Press, 1942). For Aristotle's *History of Animals,* books 7–10, I have used David Balme's Loeb Classical Library translation (Cambridge, Mass.: Harvard University Press, 1991). (In many cases, I have modified these translations.) For the rest, unless otherwise indicated, translations from the Greek are my own.

* * *

A 1997 summer stipend from the Office of Grants and Research at Seton Hall University enabled me to make a good start on this book; a sabbatical in the spring of 2001 allowed me to complete a first draft. I wish to express my gratitude to Seton Hall for its continued support of my research.

Thanks also to the staff of the University of Chicago Press—and especially David Brent and Yvonne Zipter—for their help on, and support for, this project.

Chapter 2 of this book appeared, in an earlier version, in the journal *Phronesis*. I thank Brill Publishers for permission to include that material here. In November 2002, I took part in a colloquium organized by Tara Smith and sponsored by the University of Texas at Austin Fellowship for the Study of Objectivism. My paper consisted of parts of chapters 1 and 5 of this monograph. Lesley Ann Dean-Jones, my commentator on that occasion, made a number of criticisms that improved the content of chapter 5; conversation with Allan Gotthelf, Greg Salmieri, and Tara Smith led to a number of improvements in chapter 1. I wish to thank these participants in the colloquium for their many helpful comments.

Additional (and special) thanks are due Allan Gotthelf for making available to me, prior to its publication, David Balme's *editio maior* of the Greek text of Aristotle's *History of Animals* (which Allan was at the time preparing for publication, and which has since been published by Cambridge University Press), for his comments on the entire manuscript (and especially chap. 3), and, for introducing me to the joys and brilliance of Aristotle's biology in a 1985 seminar at Georgetown University (which he co-taught with Alfonso Gomez-Lobo). Finally, I wish to thank Jim Lennox, who read the entire manuscript—some parts of it in more than one version. His detailed and intelligent comments have improved every chapter.

ABBREVIATIONS

ARISTOTLE

DA   *De anima*
EE   *Eudemian Ethics*
GA   *Generation of Animals*
GC   *Generation and Corruption*
HA   *History of Animals*
NE   *Nicomachean Ethics*
PA   *Parts of Animals*
Pol.   *Politics*
Rhet.   *Rhetoric*

LIDDELL-SCOTT-JONES

LSJ   H. G. Liddell and R. Scott, *Greek-English Lexicon,*
        rev. H. S. Jones (Oxford: Oxford University Press, 1968)

ONE

ARISTOTLE AND "IDEOLOGY"

Aristotle's remarks on females are, along with his defense of slavery, generally regarded as the nadir of his philosophy and science. The problem is not simply that he is wrong (as he was in maintaining that the sun and other celestial objects orbit the earth); nor is it simply that there are gaps in his reasoning. The problem, many believe, is that his views about the female are the product not of honest (though mistaken) science but of ideological bias—specifically, of a misogynist ideology typical of ancient Greek men.

For example, Eva Keuls, in *The Reign of the Phallus,* calls Aristotle "one of the fiercest misogynists of all times" (1993, 405). Maryanne Cline Horowitz, in her article "Aristotle and Women," refers to Aristotle as a "supposed 'empiricist'" and sees a connection between what she calls "Aristotle's biological and political sexism" (1976, 205, 207). Not only do his remarks on women represent "sex prejudice" (205), they are dangerous as well, she claims, because they are the source of "many of the standard Western arguments for the inferiority of womankind and for the political subordination of women to men in home and in society" (183).

In the same spirit (though working at a higher level of Aristotle scholarship), G. E. R. Lloyd, in *Science, Folklore and Ideology,* writes that it "is fairly evidently the case" that Aristotle's "account of women in particular and of the female sex in general provides some kind of rationalisation or accommodation of widespread Greek social attitudes" (1983, 95). A few pages later, he concludes: "The quality of Aristotle's research on the differences between the sexes is uneven and in the confrontation between theory and observational data the complexity of the latter is not allowed seriously to undermine the former. . . . Yet even if his research had been more comprehensive, careful and exact, his preconception of the superiority of the male sex would have survived intact—at least so long as he accepted the

ideological presuppositions of his contemporaries concerning the differences between men and women" (1983, 104). Malcolm Schofield, who
defends Aristotle's theory of natural slavery against the charge of ideological bias (though not the theory itself, of course), asserts that Aristotle's
remarks on women represent "a classic instance of false consciousness"
(1990, 11).

Aristotle's conception of the female is, in general and in many details,
false. But frequently, too little care is taken over rigorous scholarship on
the part of some of his fiercest critics. Often, there is little concern for what
precisely his views are on a particular issue. Nor is there much concern
with presenting support for the claim that his arguments about females are
little more than rationalization.

There is a great deal of confusion over what Aristotle says in his biological writings about females and whether what he says about them there
is ideological. This may in part be a result of the fact that, until fairly re-
cently, scholars of ancient philosophy have tended to neglect Aristotle's
biological works (the three most important being his *History of Animals,*
Parts of Animals, and *Generation of Animals*).[1] In this monograph, I investigate Aristotle's most notorious claims from the biology about females and
attempt to determine whether they are products of honest science or of
bias and ideology.

"IDEOLOGY" AND IDEOLOGICAL RATIONALIZATION

The entry on ideology in *The Encyclopedia of Philosophy* begins: "'Ideology' did not begin as a term of abuse, and in current usage it often so far
escapes any implications of exposé or denunciation that it embraces any
subjectively coherent set of political beliefs. In mid-career, however, in the
use that Karl Marx gave it, 'ideology' signified a false consciousness of
social and economic realities, a collective illusion shared by members of
a given social class."[2] The term "ideology" has at least two major senses
nowadays. First, there is a general, nonpejorative sense that is widespread
outside of academia (and, to my mind, is perfectly legitimate). For example, one common, nontechnical dictionary defines "ideology" as "the
body of doctrine or thought that guides an individual, social movement,
institution, or group."[3] In this sense, to speak of someone's ideology is in

1. See Gotthelf and Lennox 1987, 5–6.
2. Braybrooke 1967, 124–25.
3. *Random House Webster's Dictionary,* 2d ed. (1996).

no way to suggest that it was arrived at through dishonesty, evasion, bias, or rationalization. Second, there is a pejorative use of the term (derived from Marx) that is especially widespread in academic circles.

Since I am not a Marxist (neither in politics nor as an historian of ideas), in this monograph I generally avoid using "ideology" in the pejorative sense. Instead, I prefer to speak of ideological bias or rationalization. I'll be investigating whether certain claims made in Aristotle's biology are honest (however mistaken) or the result of ideological rationalization. People are capable of rationalization on all sorts of issues. A man who lies to his wife about his infidelity can, I imagine, come up with all kinds of lame arguments (for himself and anyone who asks) in defense of his actions. But it would be inaccurate, in my view, to call his ideas on marital fidelity ideologically biased.

One step closer to ideological rationalization is what I would call intellectual rationalization. This would cover rationalization in defense of one's fundamental beliefs (in contrast, say, to the narrow issue of one's marital fidelity). For example, if a person generates a host of weak "arguments" in defense of the immortality of the soul, and he does so, it turns out, not simply out of philosophical ineptness but because he wants very much to chat with dead relatives or famous dead people when he dies, that is intellectual rationalization.

What I am calling "ideological rationalization" is a subclass of intellectual rationalization, involving one's own social and political beliefs and interests. It does not refer (as "ideology" sometimes does) solely to the defense of the views of those in power. Rather, it refers to social and political beliefs, and the "arguments" in defense of those beliefs, that turn out to be (for whatever reason) mere rationalization.

Suppose we conclude that a member of the aristocracy defended monarchy, with pretty shabby arguments, because of his social class. Or suppose a wealthy heir defended capitalism with weak arguments because of his economic status. In such cases, we would surely suspect ideological bias and have real doubts about the integrity of the person and his motives in presenting such poor arguments. But in my view, it is also bias if, say, a philosopher attacks capitalism with weak arguments that are merely a cloak for his genuine motives—for example, it turns out that he condemns capitalism because doing so is the academic status quo, or fashionable among intellectuals, or out of envy for the rich and successful. Similarly, if an ancient Greek philosopher concluded—with little concern for evidence and/or with pitifully weak arguments—that women are inferior to men, and he did so in order to justify the superior social status of men, that is ideological rationalization. But in the same way, if a modern historian or classicist concludes—with little concern for evidence and with pitifully weak arguments—that certain ancient Greek philosophers and scientists were misogynist, and he does so in order to justify his reading of history, say, or his political agenda, that too is ideological rationalization.

CULTURAL CONTEXT

I do not believe that every thinker is guilty of rationalization. In fact, everyone is (or should be) capable of objectivity. (More on this later.) But this does not imply that a scientist works in a cultural vacuum, under no influence from his intellectual, historical, and social context.

There are numerous ways in which a cultural context limits or tends to limit a scientist. The nature of the debate and the key issues inherited by a scientist will tend to affect how he approaches an issue, as will the state of the evidence and the period of scientific development in which a scientist works. This last is especially important: Is science primitive or relatively advanced? Is the thinker making the first steps in a science—emerging from a culture of myth and folklore—or is he preceded by decades or centuries of sophisticated methodology and breathtaking scientific achievements? Does the thinker live in a culture in which, for example, earth, air, fire, and water are generally regarded as the basic constituents of physical reality, or is he working in the age of atomic theory and electron microscopes? Further, the nature of society and social roles—for example, the status of women—can create obstacles for the scientist. All of this is part of a thinker's cultural context.

In Aristotle's case, take for example the discussion of the female's role in generation. In part because of how the issue was treated by scientists and nonscientists before and contemporary with Aristotle, he discussed generation in part in terms of whether the female contributed seed to generation. Further, without a microscope, it was simply the case that there were certain conclusions about the nature of generation that he could not reach. And given the ancient conception of the female as inferior to the male, there may well have been pressures on Aristotle to view the issue in a certain way—pressures not exerted on a geneticist working in the twenty-first century. (Whether or to what extent the Greek conception of the female as inferior had an effect on Aristotle's conclusions about the female's role in generation is discussed in chap. 3.)

Cultural context sets limits to what a scientist can do and creates certain obstacles that may be difficult or even impossible to overcome. The important point for this study, however, is that a scientist is not trapped in this context. The content of his scientific theories is not determined or set in advance by this context. One's cultural context does not make objectivity impossible—at least not for those who aren't ideologically biased. In fact, a scientist is quite capable of radically reassessing the views of his predecessors and of his culture. A lack of objectivity is not an inevitable consequence of working in a certain cultural context; it is the result of evasion, dishonesty, or other human failings.

Schofield writes that ideological bias (what he calls "ideology") involves "false consciousness: someone holding such a belief will typically labour under a delusion or practice insincerity or both" (1990, 3). I would use stronger language: ideological bias always involves evasion and/or dishonesty—psychological or cognitive states that are under one's control. To accuse a thinker of ideological rationalization is to imply that he could have done otherwise, that he could have come to other conclusions if he had not evaded, been dishonest, engaged in rationalization, and so forth. (The difference between the Marxist sense of "ideology" and my use of "ideological rationalization" is more than mere terminology. I reject the use of "ideology" in the Marxist sense ultimately because it is rooted in Marxist determinism, which—it should be clear—I also reject.)

I maintain that "social causation"—being influenced by one's cultural context—is not automatically evidence of ideological rationalization.[4] For example, one reason that, while almost all educated people today accept the view that women can philosophize, most people living around the Mediterranean in the fourth century B.C. did not is that the latter had few if any examples of women philosophizing. If this kind of influence—that is, the enormous lack of evidence for some belief—is included in the meaning of "social causation," then in my view that, by itself, is not evidence of rationalization. So as I see it, an ancient Greek denying the possibility of female philosophers would not necessarily—or at least not obviously—involve any such "false consciousness." On the contrary, we *might* conclude, after further investigation, that a particular thinker who holds an obnoxious belief is excused of the charge of bias *because* of the cultural context within which he was working.

Of course, if a thinker is cleared of such a charge, that does not mean that his ideas were formed (or even deformed) without any influence from

4. Compare Schofield 1990, 1.

the cultural context within which he was working. We shall see that Aristotle's biology was at times influenced in this way. What I reject is the following conclusion, succinctly stated by Lloyd: "The value-laden-ness, including at times the ideological slant, of much of [Aristotle's] work in the life sciences, so far from being fortuitous, or a mere residue from traditional assumptions, corresponds to one of the primary motivations of the Aristotelian enterprise" (1983, 215). This passage makes a useful distinction between what I would consider a thinker's cultural context—from which there is usually a "residue from traditional assumptions"—and ideological rationalization, which describes a particular thinker's primary and biased motivations.[5] I hope to show—contra Lloyd and others—that although there are residues from traditional assumptions to be found in Aristotle's biology, little therein is the result of rationalization.

TESTING FOR IDEOLOGICAL RATIONALIZATION

In each of the following chapters (save the conclusion), I discuss one of Aristotle's claims (or sets of claims) from the biology about women or females generally. I usually proceed by raising two questions: (1) What exactly does Aristotle claim? (2) Is there any evidence that Aristotle's claim, and the arguments in support of it, are the product of rationalization? The first question is straightforward.[6] The second, however, raises a complex cluster of questions.

Looking for evidence of ideological rationalization involves, at some level, an investigation into the motives that led a person to conclude what he did.[7] There are two pitfalls here that need to be avoided. First, moral courtesy (for lack of a better expression) demands that we avoid psycholo-

---

5. There is surely a difference between a thinker who consciously and maliciously "massages" his arguments and observations so as to reach, inevitably, an already-held misogynist conclusion and a thinker who is careless in accepting and applying certain widespread negative assumptions about females. In fact, many who assert that Aristotle's biology is ideologically motivated or driven would claim that he does not fall under the first category of thinker. For purposes of this study, however, I do not make a distinction between the two types of thought processes, since both count as ideological rationalization.

6. It is straightforward in the sense that it is clear what is meant in asking the question. I do not mean that answering this question is in every case straightforward.

7. This does not necessarily involve an investigation into the *specific* motives of a thinker; but at the very least it involves an investigation into whether—judging from his arguments (or lack thereof) and assumptions—a thinker was motivated by a rational desire to know reality objectively or by a desire to support some outlook, agenda, or position.

gizing—guessing at what psychological state (or problem) might have led Aristotle to hold a given position.[8] This is best avoided by not assuming too hastily that if Aristotle is mistaken on some issue—even on an issue with social implications—it must be owing to intellectual dishonesty.

A second and related pitfall is the precariousness of the attempt to test for rationalization. We lack direct access to the beliefs and motives of a thinker, and especially an ancient one, who is not around to discuss his ideas. It is difficult to determine what may have led a person to hold a particular idea; the often sketchy evidence exacerbates this difficulty. The best approach that I have found—one that avoids psychologizing while providing a pretty reliable guide with which to investigate ideological bias— was developed by Charles Kahn (1990, 29). I present his "ideology test" here, though I have revised it somewhat.[9]

> An ideological interpretation of some claim is appropriate when the following conditions hold:
> 1. the claim does in fact tend to promote a specific ideological agenda or justify social interests (i.e., interests of class, social position, gender, etc.);
> 2. the claim exhibits one of the following two features:
>   a. it rests upon arbitrary or implausible assumptions and/or is supported by unusually bad arguments;
>   b. it conflicts with other fundamental principles held by the same thinker.

Let me explain each of these points in greater detail and as they apply to Aristotle's claims about females.

8. Rand (1988, 24) writes: "Psychologizing consists in condemning or excusing specific individuals on the grounds of their psychological problems, real or invented, in the absence of or contrary to factual evidence." I regard misogyny, the hatred of women, as a pretty low psychological state—one that should not be attributed to a person without ample evidence.

9. I cannot say whether Kahn would agree with any of my revisions to his "test" (my language, not his)—or, for that matter, with any of my applications of it in this book. In fairness to Kahn, I provide his original presentation of it here: "An ideological interpretation is appropriate when the following conditions hold: (I) the doctrine in question does in fact tend to justify such social interests [i.e., the interests of a thinker's class, social position, gender, etc.] and (II) the doctrine exhibits one or more of the three following features: (a) it rests upon assumptions that seem arbitrary or implausible, (b) it is supported by unusually bad arguments, and (c) it conflicts with other fundamental principles held by the same philosopher" (1990, 29).

Point 1. The claim does in fact tend to justify the interests of men
at the expense of the interests of women.

Although some might hold that any negative view of females fits this description, I think it would be well to consider whether a given negative claim in fact supports the interests of men at the expense of the interests of women. For example, one might posit that Aristotle's claim that females contribute less to generation than men would—to the extent to which his works contribute to this position becoming or remaining accepted—undercut how women are viewed and treated. But this connection is by no means clear. The critic of Aristotle must show how Aristotle's claim would lead to some kind of injustice or mistreatment. Nevertheless, I find this tricky territory, so if some claim of Aristotle's seems to fulfill the requirements of point 1, I proceed to point 2.

It is worth stressing that point 2 is necessary. Some might claim that if any idea meets the conditions stated in point 1, then that is, ipso facto, evidence of ideological bias. But such a move is too hasty. The most that fulfilling point 1 might do is raise, in certain cases, the possibility of an ideological interpretation; it certainly does not confirm it. As I hope will become clear, we need to answer the questions posed in point 2 to be justified in concluding that a thinker's arguments are in fact a rationalization for some ideological conclusion.[10]

I believe that there are some inherently dishonest beliefs—beliefs that so fly in the face of the facts that, putting aside mentally disabled or extremely stupid people, such a belief can be said to be so obviously wrong that only a dishonest person could accept it, that is, that accepting such a belief requires dishonesty, evasion, rationalization. For example, take the belief in the intellectual superiority of one race over another or of men over women. In such cases, and certainly by the twentieth century, the belief itself gives you all you need in order to accuse a thinker of ideological rationalization (and more). But even here, as noted above, cultural context makes a difference. What is obviously true to us—for example, women can philosophize—may not have been obvious to a fourth-century B.C. Greek. (Note that I take "obvious" here not as a sign of the predominant ideology in a particular culture but to refer to the abundance of actual evidence in support of a belief.) If one wants to demonstrate that it was also obvious to

---

10. The type of work one is examining makes a difference. That is, I believe one is more likely to regard as worthy of consideration an ideologically oriented passage appearing in a biological text than the same line appearing in a work on politics (the purpose of which is to present ideological views).

such a Greek that women can philosophize, if only he tried to see it, one will need to go on to point 2.

Before turning to point 2, I should mention that I assume that we can tell the difference between good and bad arguments and between bad and unusually bad arguments. I do not regard the standards for determining the merit of an argument to be arbitrary or culturally dependent. Clearly, I cannot discuss these issues here or even present a set of specific guidelines. I will instead deal with these issues as they arise in the chapters of this book. But consider this example, which contrasts a bad and an unusually bad argument. If a fifth-century B.C. Greek thinker did a survey of all ancient Mediterranean cities and civilizations and concluded that on the basis of the results of this survey, women are incapable of philosophizing, we should conclude that although his case is not entirely without merit (he did, after all, do some research) his reasoning is not terribly sound. Now contrast this with a fifth-century B.C. Greek thinker who claims that women cannot philosophize and does so because everyone he knows believes this and/or as a result of evading some solid evidence to the contrary. I would regard his "reasoning" as unusually bad—"reasoning" that is much more ideologically suspect than the argument of the first thinker in this example. (This is not to deny that there are tricky, borderline cases.)

*Point 2a. The claim rests on arbitrary or implausible assumptions
and/or is supported by unusually bad arguments.*

Disagreements are always possible among individuals, and it is mistaken to assume, whenever we encounter faulty reasoning, that the author of an argument in defense of a position we reject must have been motivated by some kind of bias. If we find that a thinker holds a belief that fulfills the requirement of point 1 and that his reasoning is flawed, we must next ask: How flawed?

By "arbitrary and implausible," I mean that the claim seems arbitrary or implausible in the cultural and historical context of ancient Greece. If a scientist today rejected evolution or said that the earth was flat and at rest at the center of the universe, we might suspect some kind of (religious) bias—assumptions about the creation and nature of the universe that are arbitrary or implausible and thus immune from rational inquiry. But we should not immediately come to the same conclusion about an ancient biologist or astronomer holding similar views, for his basic methodological assumptions may be quite sound. Of course, one can almost always invent some kind of ideologically or otherwise-biased motivation for a scientific or philosophical position. For example, it is conceivable that some ancient

Greek advocate of the view that the earth is fixed at the center of the universe—without divine support—might have adopted his view not because of compelling evidence and strong arguments but out of a nihilist desire to undercut the traditional Olympian religion and morality of the times. Inventing an ideological scenario is easy; the important question is, does the evidence support such a scenario? We must look at the arguments presented before judging how good or bad they are (however mistaken their conclusions).

If a philosopher or scientist today downplayed the role of females in generation—or even worse, argued that women were incapable of philosophy or political rule on the assumption that women are inferior—we would immediately reject the assumption as baseless and assume some kind of bias, and with a great deal of justification. But we should not immediately assume bias on the part of an ancient Greek thinker who made such claims. For ancient Greek biologists lacked a microscope and a long history of biological research to build on. And it may very well be the case that, in ancient Mediterranean cultures around the time of Aristotle, women (with some very rare exceptions) neither philosophized nor ruled. Before we could conclude bias, we would have to ask: What arguments were used to defend the assumption? How good were they? What was known at the time? How extensive was the research? And so on. Only in this way could we determine whether a thinker was honestly mistaken or engaging in ideological rationalization.

As for the arguments a thinker employs to support his positions, I take "unusually bad" to refer roughly to a lack of evidence, gaps in argumentation, non sequiturs, logical fallacies, and so forth that are so egregious that it is hard to imagine a person (and especially a great mind) committing such errors innocently, sincerely, and without evasion.

Point 2b. The claim conflicts with other fundamental
principles held by Aristotle.

Aristotle, the discoverer of the law of noncontradiction, was well aware that contradiction is a sign that something is not right—that falsehood is present. Avoiding contradiction is the essence of logic. So, if two or more claims from among a person's set of ideas clash (and were not held or put forward at different times), we must conclude that at least one claim from among that person's set of ideas is false.[11] But can we conclude that the contradic-

---

11. Since Jaeger (1948), emphasis is sometimes placed on chronology in the study of Aristotle. But chronology rarely plays a role in the study of Aristotle's remarks on females in his

tion is maintained in order to avoid arriving at a conclusion that, for ideological reasons, one refuses to accept? As in the previous points, we should not assume prejudice too hastily. To justify an accusation of ideological bias, we must show that the breach in logic is so obvious that, again, it is hard to imagine an intelligent person holding such a contradiction innocently or sincerely.

DIALECTIC

One might argue that such tests for ideological bias in Aristotle's science are useless because they ignore the nature of Aristotle's dialectic, which—the objection would maintain—seems built to lead to ideological conclusions.

In *Topics* 1.1, Aristotle tells us that a deduction (συλλογισμός) is dialectic if it "reasons from noted opinions" (ἐνδόξων συλλογιζόμενος) (100a29–30). He describes these noted opinions or *endoxa* as those opinions "that are accepted by everyone or by most people or by the wise—i.e., by all [of the wise], or by most of them, or by the most famous and reputable of them" (100b21–23). In *NE* 7.1, there is a famous passage that seems to describe this method: "We must, as in other cases, set out the appearances [φαινόμενα], and first going through the puzzles, in this way prove, if possible, all of the noted opinions [ἔνδοξα] about these affections, but if not all, then most of them and the most important. For if the problems are solved and the noted opinions are left, we will have proven the case sufficiently" (1145b2–7). Dialectic is not Aristotle's only method, but it is a prominent one in his philosophy. Not surprisingly, it is sometimes viewed as a conservative method, the use of which makes it highly unlikely that Aristotle could go beyond the "noted opinions," thus making him trapped in the ideology of his times. Schofield writes:

> Whether the endoxic method is conservative or merely elastic it can offer little resistance to popular ideology. Either way it fails to provide adequate *stimulus* to question whether what we take to be "our lived experience of the world" (e.g. "our" perception of slaves as inferior) is really experience, or even if it is, whether that experience might not be a function of social circumstances which could and conceivably should be different from what they are. . . . To be sure, the method accords reason a critical role. But

---

biological writings. (On the development of Aristotle's biology, see Balme [1987, 17–18; 1991, 1–30] and Lennox [1996].)

Aristotle's discussions of the method leave the critical function theoretically underdescribed and indeed undernourished, so to speak. Is it any surprise that in practice its radical potential (which on a conservative interpretation of the method is in principle more limited in any case than Nussbaum would like) goes largely unrealized? The endoxic method, then, leaves its practitioners all too prone to succumb to popular ideology.[12] (1990, 7–8)

I cannot begin to deal with the thicket of problems involved in attempting to present a clear picture of Aristotle's dialectic or go into the numerous interpretations of it that have been offered. I shall simply make two brief points, one about Aristotle's biology, the other about his practical philosophy.

1. The focus of this monograph is on Aristotle's biology, which contains the majority of his comments on the female. I cannot here sufficiently answer the question: In what way, if any, does Aristotle employ dialectic in his biology? I shall mention only that I believe Robert Bolton is probably right in arguing that the empirical methodology of Aristotle's biology conforms to the method described in the *Posterior Analytics* and that this method is not dialectic.[13] Dialectic, he argues, does have a role to play, but it is preliminary, not primary.

Discussing Aristotle's critique of the "pangenesis" theory of generation and the role it plays in Aristotle's discussion of seed (σπέρμα), Bolton writes: "The function of the dialectical discussion here is thus to indicate where we stand as a result of a review of received opinions in which the more generally apparent and accredited are allowed to take precedence over others where there is a conflict. As such, dialectic serves here only to fix on what is most obvious to us about sperma and nothing beyond" (1987, 155). To go beyond what is most obvious—for example, to inquire further about the nature of seed—requires empirical demonstration, not dialectic.

But whether or not this interpretation of the role of dialectic in the

12. "Our lived experience of the world" is a quote from Nussbaum (1982, 292). Here is the full passage: "The method does not make discoveries, radical departures, or sharp changes of position impossible, either in science or in ethics. What it does do is to explain to us how any radical or new view must commend itself to our attention: by giving evidence of its superior ability to integrate and organise features of our lived experience of the world." I agree with the spirit of this passage but not with Nussbaum's interpretation of Aristotle's dialectic generally. As I see it, her claims to the contrary notwithstanding, she replaces Aristotle's realism and objectivity with a kind of Kantian intersubjectivity.

13. Bolton 1987; see also Gotthelf 1987b; Lennox 2001b, chaps. 1–2.

biology is correct, what is most important—and I believe obvious—is that Aristotle was quite able to reject the "noted opinions" on some topic and replace them with a position that he thought was supported by observation. Here are some examples from the *Generation of Animals:* Aristotle rejects the claims of Ktesias of Knidos concerning the semen of elephants (2.2.735b37–736a5); he rejects the theory of Democritus et al., according to which the external parts of the embryo are formed first (2.4.740a13–19); he rejects the common view that hyenas are hermaphrodites (3.6.757a2–13). In each of these cases, his rejection is explicitly based on observation.[14] In some cases, his observation-based rejection of a theory relies on dissections: for example, his rejection of the view (of Democritus and of the Hippocratic writers?) that children are nourished in the womb by sucking on a bit of flesh (2.7.746a19–22) and his rejection of Empedocles' explanation of the formation of twins (4.1.764a33–b3).[15]

Moreover, if Aristotle does accept a theory—or creates an original theory of his own—he considers it provisional if it is not sufficiently based on the facts. In *GA* 3.10, he writes: "So, this seems to be the way things are concerning the generation of bees, judging from theory and from what are thought to be the facts about them. The facts, however, have not yet been sufficiently grasped; but if they are ever grasped, then we must rely on sense perception more than on theories and on theories only if what they set forth agrees with what has been observed" (760b27–33).[16] Clearly, in discussing the passages on females in Aristotle's biology, we need not worry that his methodology makes ideological bias inescapable.

Of course, we must always check on content. Aristotle was capable of accepting some positions without adequate evidence and with insufficient reasoning. For example, in the *Generation of Animals,* he seems to accept a water test for fertility that has more in common with folklore and old wives' tales than with science (2.7.747a3–22). But such slips are rare and not fundamental.

2. Although the passages on women from the *Politics* and from Aristotle's ethical works are scattered and do not form a sustained argument

14. See also *GA* 1.15.720b32–36, 2.1.734a16–22, 2.8.748a7–20, 3.5.756a2–5, 3.5.756a30–34, 5.8.788b9–29.

15. On the view that children are nourished in the womb by sucking on a bit of flesh as possibly originating with Democritus and the Hippocratic writers, see Peck (1942, 240). See also, on the formation of twins, *GA* 4.4.771b32–33. From the *History of Animals,* Bolton mentions 3.2.511b13–23 and 3.3.513a8–15, to which I would add 1.491b28 and 3.1.510a12–35.

16. For two other examples of Aristotle's hesitation about some claim due to the lack of reliable observations, see *GA* 2.5.741a32–37 and 2.7.746b4–7.

about the nature of women, they may well be parts of dialectical arguments.[17] And Aristotle's arguments in his ethical and political works can be epistemologically conservative. For example, in his critique of Plato's *Republic* in the *Politics*, he writes: "One should not ignore this point, that it is necessary to pay attention to the great amount of time and the many years during which it would not have gone unnoticed if these [measures, i.e., those establishing a communism of property] were fine. For nearly everything has been discovered" (2.5.1264a1–4). Note, however, that this was one argument in a series of more than a half dozen against the communism of property.[18] So far as I know, Aristotle never argues for something simply based on the way things have always been.

Dialectic does tend to make Aristotle's epistemology too conservative and vulnerable not necessarily to ideological bias but to an improper reliance on cultural norms as empirical evidence. Since I sometimes (though not often) touch on what Aristotle says outside the biological writings, we need to keep his appeals to *endoxa* in mind. But I do not think bias is an inescapable part of his philosophy and science. So I proceed in each case using the test for ideological rationalization outlined above.

THE "MYTH OF OBJECTIVITY"

One might object that regardless of the nature of Aristotle's method(s), the investigation at the heart of this monograph is completely misguided because objectivity is a myth: all philosophy and science is rationalization and the product of ideology.[19] One can attribute such a position to Paul

---

17. As Schofield points out (1990, 8–9), dialectic is not the method of *Pol.*, bk. 1 (which contains the most extensive remarks about women in the *Politics*). He writes:

Aristotle does not follow the canonical method of *endoxa* in his treatment of slavery. In [*Pol.*, bk. 1] Aristotle (1) announces at the outset that he will pursue what is quite evidently an entirely different method: a method of analysis (1252a17–23); (2) follows this method in his discussions both of slavery and of household management [and, I would add, of women (though there is no sustained discussion of women in *Pol.*, bk. 1, as there is of slavery and household management)]; (3) points out from time to time that he is following it (1253b1–8 and I 8; 1256a1–3; cf. 1254a20 ff). Most of the opinions of others on these topics that he cites in the course of [*Pol.*, bk. 1] he rejects as erroneous.

18. For Aristotle's arguments against the Platonic communism of property, see Mayhew (1997b, chap. 5).

19. Lloyd seems to approach this view but does not quite reach it. He writes: "All ancient science is, no doubt, ideological in the sense that the different groups of those who engaged in various types of inquiry were more or less actively engaged in legitimating their own positions. But not all of ancient science was seen as in the service of a morality or directly linked

Feyerabend, who sought to exorcise the demons, as he saw them, of reason and objectivity from philosophy and science.[20] "Scientific method," Feyerabend claims, "is but an ornament which makes us forget that a position of 'anything goes' has in fact been adopted" (1970, 229). "The similarities between science and myth," he says, "are indeed astonishing" (1975, 298). This last is not a critique of what he sees as the woeful state of science but is simply part of the nature of any science. Though he does not speak of Aristotle's views on females, I suspect Feyerabend would have concluded without reading a word of Aristotle's biology that his "science" cannot be the product of an attempt to know the world objectively through a rational methodology. (And if not that, what is the most likely alternative source of Aristotle's "science" but his own prejudices?)

This outlook is quite prominent in gender studies. For example, the French philosopher Luce Irigaray, who is well known in feminist and continental philosophy circles, writes: "*Every* piece of knowledge is produced by subjects in a given historical context. Even if that knowledge aims to be objective, even if its techniques are designed to ensure objectivity, science *always* displays certain choices, certain exclusions, and these are particularly determined by the sex of the scholars involved" (1993, 104, emphasis added).[21] The assumption that objectivity is a myth gives Irigaray a great deal of freedom—for example, in her "reading" of the works of others. Consider this passage from Aristotle's *Physics* 4.1: "Further, too, if it is itself an existent, it will be somewhere. Zeno's difficulty demands an explanation: for if everything that exists has a place, place too will have a place, and so on *ad infinitum*" (209a23–26).[22] Irigaray's comments on this passage have little to do with its content but then "anything goes" (to use Feyerabend's language). For instance, she writes: "I go on a quest through an indefinite number of bodies, through nature, through God, for the body that once served as place for me, where I (male/female) was able to stay contained, enveloped. Given that, as far as man is concerned, the issue is to separate the first and the last place. . . . As for woman, she is place. Does she have to locate herself in bigger and bigger places?" (1998, 41–42). And so on, ad nauseam.

---

to a notion of the good life, let alone geared to underpinning the moral and political attitudes implied in the dominant ideology" (1983, 215).

20. See, esp., Feyerabend 1975, 1987. For a brief but good critique of Feyerabend, see Sokal and Bricmont (1998, 78–85) and, esp., Lennox (1981).

21. See also Rosser 1992, 54.

22. This is the translation (from the rev. Oxford translation of Aristotle) used in Irigaray (1998).

These passages may represent an extreme example of the result of rejecting the possibility of objectivity; but the idea that objectivity is a myth —that the best we can hope for is some kind of intersubjectivity—has been an increasingly influential idea since Kant and today is ubiquitous. It is well beyond the scope of this study to discuss the nature and validity of objectivity and to explode the myth that objectivity is a myth. What I can do is point out that the approach of Feyerabend, Irigaray, et al. is utterly self-defeating and thus need not be taken seriously.

But let us for a moment take seriously Irigaray's claim that no "piece of knowledge" can be objectively established. To be consistent, we would have to conclude that this is true of her claim itself: she cannot maintain that as a result of her unbiased, objective, methodically sound research into the history of science, she can demonstrate that "even if its techniques are designed to ensure objectivity, science always displays certain choices . . . [that] are particularly determined by the sex of the scholars involved." If she does make such a claim to objectivity, then she is guilty of a contradiction—of saying, in effect, "an intellectual inquiry cannot escape bias and my intellectual inquiry escaped bias."[23] But if she does not, why should we take her admittedly nonobjective, sexually biased views on science seriously? She would have to say, if sincere, that she did not come to any objective conclusions about the history of gender and science; rather, she concluded what she did because she was motivated by the desire, say, to empower women. But if that was her motivation, why should anyone (who does not share her biases) be interested in reading what she wrote about the history of science? And why did she write what she wrote (rather than writing, say, a defense of—or, since that's not really possible on her approach, a description of her feelings about—the empowerment of women)?[24]

23. On this contradiction in Irigaray's reading of Aristotle, see Freeland (1998b, 85–86).

24. For a good critique of Irigaray, see Sokal and Bricmont (1998, 106–23). My objection to Irigaray can be leveled against Feyerabend as well. If he has bid farewell to reason and objectivity and believes science can proceed without empirical evidence, what does this say about his own work? He cannot honestly and consistently claim to have rationally and objectively arrived at his subjectivist, antiscience, and antireason philosophy. The best he could honestly do is claim: "For reasons of my own having nothing to do with reason, objectivity or method, I have come to conclude what I have." Morbid curiosity might lead one to guess at his motives, but that is not enough to justify taking his ideas seriously as an attack on objectivity and reason.

Louis Sass, in *Madness and Modernism*, provides a possible clue to Feyerabend's motives: "It is only in the modernist era that we find artworks whose most central attitude is not to communicate or to celebrate, but to pour scornful laughter on the whole of existence"

We must begin with the assumption that objective knowledge is possible (though obviously not automatic): that it was possible for Aristotle in his work in biology in the fourth century B.C. and that it is possible (or may be possible, depending on the state of the evidence) to know whether Aristotle was guilty of ideological rationalization when he wrote, in his biological works, about females.

A NOTE ON THE SCOPE OF THIS STUDY

This monograph has two limitations in scope that should be clear by now but that I want to make explicit and explain. First, my aim in this chapter was to briefly defend the view that despite not working in a cultural vacuum, a scientist is capable of objectivity and even a radical departure from his cultural context. It was not my purpose to contribute directly to the substantial literature on ideology and science. I have therefore limited myself to explaining my outlook and providing sufficient support for what I call the test for ideological rationalization. One can disagree with my approach to the relationship between science and ideology and/or my evaluation of Aristotle's biology (whether or to what extent he is guilty of ideological rationalization) and still find informative my discussion of what Aristotle says about the female in his biology.

Second, this book focuses on Aristotle's biological writings. It is not a study of what he has to say about women in his moral and political works. I am here interested in Aristotle the scientist. I do not believe there is much of a connection between his biology on the one hand and his moral and political philosophy on the other. For example, Aristotle's notion that women are not sufficiently intelligent to rule in the city is not, I believe, the result of conclusions he came to in his biology. Rather, I suspect that in his moral and political philosophy he simply came to conclusions based on empirical observations of women at the time and in the place in which he lived. There are interesting questions about the nature of his views and how objective or ideological he was in arriving at them; but I think the much more interesting issues reside in his biological works. I therefore make use of Aristotle's ethical writings (e.g., in chap. 6) only when doing so can be connected to, and contributes to, something he says in his biological writings.

* * *

(1992, 36). The same can be said about postmodern philosophy, of which Feyerabend could serve as a symbol.

I do not believe that the primary goal of historians of philosophy and science is to sniff out ideological bias. The search for "ideology" is, unfortunately, too often an opportunity to attack gratuitously the motives and character of thinkers who defend views (and especially political views) with which the attacker disagrees. I agree with Jonathan Barnes's claim that "the discovery of ideological bias in ancient texts itself more often manifests prejudice than profundity" (1984a, 9). Rather, historians of ideas should be concerned primarily with such questions as: What explicit views did a given philosopher hold? What arguments did he present in their defense? Are these good arguments and defensible philosophical positions? What is the historical and cultural context in which this philosopher worked? What philosophical influences were there on this thinker? What influences did he have on subsequent philosophers? And so on. In this monograph, I hope to answer some of these questions, in passing, on some issues in Aristotle's biology.

Given the primary aim of the historian of philosophy, why undertake this study? In investigating possible ideological bias in Aristotle's remarks in his biology on females, my motivation is reactive. I am responding to claims—often inadequately supported—about Aristotle's misogyny and ideology. As such, I think it is a worthwhile study.

In most of the following chapters, I apply the test for ideological rationalization to some of Aristotle's claims about females. In chapter 2, I begin with a set of narrow claims about entomology—the most famous being that the leader of the bees is a king bee, not a queen bee. Next, I move to three sets of claims about females generally. In chapter 3, I investigate Aristotle's beliefs about the female contribution to generation. Chapter 4 deals with Aristotle's infamous assertion that females are, as it were, mutilated males and with the related analogy he sees between women and eunuchs. In chapter 5, I look at an assortment of seemingly bizarre remarks about physical differences between males and females, for example, that females have fewer teeth than males. Chapter 6 consists of a discussion of Aristotle's claim that females are softer and less spirited than males and with some related statements about the character of females. Chapter 7 provides a summary and conclusion.

TWO

Aristotle's politics, moral philosophy, psychology, and embryology have all been chastised for being drenched in ideological—and particularly gender —bias. But surely, recent arrivals into the wonders of Aristotle's biology might conclude, his entomology (a rather small part of his biology) has remained untouched by such suspicions.[1] Not so. In this chapter, I investigate three entomological claims of Aristotle that touch on his views on gender and whether or to what extent they are ideological. Of these three claims, two have been criticized as gender biased, and of these two, one is quite infamous: his claim that the leader of the bees—what we call the queen bee—is a king bee.

KING BEES AND MOTHER WASPS

Aristotle notes in *HA* 5.21 that the large bees we today call the queens are "called 'mothers' [μητέρες] by some" (553a29), but he himself certainly accepted the more widespread usage and refers to such bees as the kings (οἱ βασιλεῖς) or the so-called kings (οἱ καλούμενοι βασιλεῖς).[2] (See his two main discussions of bees: *HA* 8 (9).40 and *GA* 3.10.)[3]

1. I use "entomology" as a convenient label for what I cover in this chapter. But note that Aristotle himself did not divide up his biological science by animal kinds in this way.

2. On "kings" having been the more widespread term for the leaders of the bees, see Hudson-Williams (1935, 2–4) and Davies and Kathirithamby (1986, 62).

It is unclear whom Aristotle has in mind when he refers to those who call the leaders of the bees "mothers" (see Hudson-Williams 1935, 4), though Xenophon considered the bee leaders female. See *Oeconomicus* 7.17, 32–33, 38, and Pomeroy (1994, 276–79), but cf. *Oeconomicus* 7.39 and see Hudson-Williams (1935, 3).

3. The modern ordering of books 7–9 is not the original manuscript order but was

But why would Aristotle call the queen bee a king?[4]

As perhaps comes as no surprise, some scholars suspect Aristotle is guilty of ideological rationalization. Simon Byl writes: "À la tête de la ruche, le biologiste place des rois: ὁ ἡγεμών, ὁ βασιλεύς. Cette erreur . . . s'explique par le préjugé de l'infériorité de la femme et de la femelle en général" (1975, 342). Similarly, Sarah Pomeroy writes: "Aristotle, unlike Xenophon, consistently refers to the leaders [of the bees] as male. Misogyny coupled with the Greek tradition of seeing analogies between human society and the hive affected Aristotle's view of the sex of the bees" (1994, 279). Malcolm Davies and Jeyaraney Kathirithamby, discussing the king bee, write that "it is hard not to feel that anti-female prejudice has played its part in determining even the views of Aristotle" (1986, 63).

Jonathan Barnes gives a good summary of how one might arrive at such an interpretation (which is not Barnes's own) of Aristotle's claim that the leader of the bees is male: "Sexual bias has been more confidently diagnosed . . . [in the case of] the bee. Aristotle held that the 'leaders' of the hive were male. His view had a lasting hold on zoologists, and it contributed not a little to political metaphor. But it reflects nothing but ideological prejudice. Had Aristotle lived in a matriarchical society, she would have known that the leaders were female" (1984a, 9).[5]

Before we can test for bias, we must ask: What precisely are Aristotle's views on this topic? Did he conclude that the leader of the bees is male, and did he do so because he automatically assumes that rulers must be male?

---

established by Theodore of Gaza in the fifteenth century. (See Balme 1991, 18–19.) Balme has restored the manuscript order of these books, and I follow him throughout this monograph. The designation "8 (9)" refers to book 8 in the manuscript order and book 9 in the modern.

4. Aristotle believes that the bee is a kind of insect and that this kind can be further divided into three "subkinds": kings, bees, and drones. Note that Aristotle uses the same name for bees in general and for one subkind of bee (those that are neither kings nor drones and that for clarity's sake I call worker bees). It is not unusual for Aristotle to use the same name for a general class and for a subclass. (For example: *NE* 6.8.1141b29–33, where "practical intelligence" [φρόνησις] refers to both a broad class and to one of the four subclasses [practical intelligence concerning oneself]—the three others being household management, legislation, and political science; *PA* 1.4 and 2.8, where τὰ ὄστρεα [usually translated "oyster"] can refer to either a broad class of shellfish [see 644b11] or one kind of animal within this class [see 654a1–5].)

5. The passage continues: "That is speculation. Against it speaks the fact that Aristotle reached his view about the leader bees after long argument." Barnes supports this claim and then concludes: "It is merely impudent to dismiss all that as so much rationalisation and to wheel on sexual bias in its place" (1984a, 9).

To answer these questions, I think it helps to look at Aristotle's discussion of wasps (οἱ σφῆκες) in *HA* 8 (9).41. Here are three passages from that chapter:

1. Some of them [the wild wasps, οἱ ἄγριοι] are mothers [or wombs, μῆτραι] while others are workers, just as in the tamer [wasps] (627b31–33).[6]

2. By the end of autumn there are many large wasp combs, in which the leader [ὁ ἡγεμών], the so-called mother [ἡ καλουμένη μήτρα], no longer generates worker wasps but mothers (628a16–18).

3. The mother is broad and heavy, fatter and larger than the worker wasp, and because of its weight it is not very strong with respect to flying. . . . The so-called mothers are present in most wasp combs. There is disagreement over whether they have stings or are stingless; but it is likely that just as in the case of the leaders of the bees [ὥσπερ οἱ τῶν μελιττῶν ἡγεμόνες], they have them but neither stick them out nor strike (628a30–b3).

Aristotle calls the wasp that corresponds to the king bee a mother, notes a similarity between the mother wasp and the king bee with respect to their stings, and maintains that these mothers are the leaders of the wasps. And it is worth noting that *HA* 8 (9).41 directly follows the discussion of bees (in chap. 40), just as the brief discussion of wasps at the end of *GA* 3.10 (see 761a2–11) directly follows the *Generation of Animals'* discus-

---

6. In a note on this passage, Balme writes that μῆτραι (which he translates "women") "usually means 'wombs' but is also used by metaphor and synecdoche" (1991, 369). A word search of Aristotle's corpus reveals that outside of his discussion of wasps, μήτρα does mean "womb." A word search of works of others besides Aristotle (and from before his death) reveals that among the writings that have survived, no one else used μήτρα to refer to the leaders of wasps. But Aristotle's occasional use of "the so-called mother" (ἡ καλουμένη μήτρα; see e.g. *HA* 8 (9).628a18) indicates that the term was in use and was not his own invention, though how common this usage was is unknown. Hesychius of Alexandria, in his lexicon (ca. fifth century A.D.), gives four uses of μήτρα, the first being εἶδος σφηκός ("kind of wasp"), though Aristotle could have been his sole source. (The fourth usage is ἡ τῆς γυναικός: "the [μήτρα] of the woman," i.e., the womb. The other two uses he mentions are irrelevant here.)

I follow Balme and others and translate μήτρα as "mother." This seems to me less odd than calling a leader of the wasps "womb" or "womb wasp" and not such a stretch as "queen wasp" (which we find in LSJ, s.v. μήτρα [3.3]).

Aristotle held that the wasp is a kind of insect and that this kind can be further divided into two subkinds: mothers and workers. He sometimes used his term for wasps in general to refer to the workers. In such cases, I use "worker wasp" to avoid confusion.

sion of bees. So, in passages directly following his discussions of bees, Aristotle seems willing to recognize female leaders in animals extremely close to bees. (Wasps and bees fall under the same unnamed kind; see *HA* 8 [9].40.623b5–10.) Yet it makes no sense to say that Aristotle was ideologically motivated in the one case but not in the other. What would be the motivation, ideologically, to call queen bees "kings" (presumably against the evidence or with insufficient evidence) and shortly thereafter to call the leaders of the wasps "mothers" or "wombs"?

This is a fair question—one that those who claim to sense a strong whiff of bias in Aristotle's account of the bees should be aware of and, in my view, cannot sufficiently answer. But it turns out that this picture is too simple. Aristotle's views on the leaders of the bees and the leaders of the wasps are much more complex. Yet his actual views are nevertheless just as inconsistent with an ideological interpretation. For the assumption so far has been that Aristotle believes that the king bees are male and the mother wasps female. But in fact, he holds that the king bees are not male (or female) and that the mother wasps are not (exclusively) female.[7]

Aristotle discusses the generation of bees primarily in *GA* 3.10. He opens by saying that the generation of bees is a "great puzzle" (πολλὴν ἀπορίαν) and that there are many different theories on this issue (759a8–24, and see *HA* 5.21.553a17–18). He systematically goes through and rejects the opposing theories of bee generation (759a24–b27) and concludes that only one possibility remains: generation without copulation (as occurs, he says, among some kinds of fish).[8] The king bees, he says, are in a sense both male and female (like plants), though neither term is really applicable. The king bees generate both the other king bees and the worker bees, and the worker bees generate the drones, all without copulation (see 759b27–760a31). So Aristotle accepts the most common name for what he also calls the leaders of the bees, namely, "king bees," though he argues that each king bee is both male and female (or neither).[9]

---

7. I here follow Aristotle's use of "male" and "female": a male animal is one that generates in another; a female animal is one that generates in itself. (See *GA* 1.2.716a13–15; cf. *HA* 1.3.489a10–12.)

8. For example, he rejects the idea that some bees are male and some female on the grounds that no bees (he claims) have ever been observed copulating (*GA* 3.10.759b15–23).

9. Aristotle refers to the leaders of the bees as both the kings (οἱ βασιλεῖς) and the so-called kings (οἱ καλούμενοι βασιλεῖς). One might think he uses "so-called" to distance himself from the term "king bees" but that need not be the case. (In fact, "what are called kings" may capture the Greek better than "so-called kings.") Aristotle sometimes uses "so-called" for

At the end of *GA* 3.10, Aristotle turns to a discussion of the generation of wasps. He writes: "The so-called mothers generate. . . , but [unlike the bees] they generate by copulating with each other, for their coupling *has often been observed*" (761a6–8). The mother wasps generate both the other mother wasps and the worker wasps (see *HA* 8 [9].41.628a10–18), and they do so by copulating with each other. Obviously, some mother wasps are male, and others are female.[10] So Aristotle accepts (at least provisionally) a name that was in use for the leaders of the wasps, namely "mother wasps" (or "womb wasps"), though he thinks some mother wasps are male and others female.

According to some scholars, Aristotle is blind to, or distorts, the truth because of his biases concerning women. One manifestation of this bias, it is claimed, is that Aristotle calls what we know to be the queen bee a king. But this criticism of Aristotle makes no sense. For this interpretation to be plausible, Aristotle would have to have concluded (no matter what the evidence) that wasp leaders and bee leaders are both kings. But each bee leader is both male and female (or neither), on his view, though he follows convention and calls them all kings; and some wasp leaders are male and some female, on his view, though he seems to follow (a) convention and calls them all mothers.

A major problem with those who find Aristotle guilty of gender bias here is that they disregard his concern for observation and his reluctance to go beyond what the evidence tells us about bees and wasps. Note (1) that in *HA* 8 (9).40–41, there is constant reference to what has (and has not) been observed and to what "they" (in most cases, the beekeepers, οἱ μελ-λιττουργοί) say; and (2) that in *GA* 3.10 (in a passage quoted in chap. 1),

---

terms he clearly accepts. For example, his term for the female's contribution to generation (among blooded animals) is *katamenia,* though he at least once refers to it as the so-called *katamenia* (τῶν καλουμένων καταμηνίων; *GA* 1.19.727a1–2). In addition, see LSJ, s.v. καλέω (2.2: passive), which even states: "almost = εἰμί."

10. Beavis misses this point (1988, 191). On Aristotle's reference to the leaders of the wasps as both the mothers (αἱ μῆτραι) and the so-called mothers (αἱ μῆτραι καλούμενη), see the preceding note.

Note that Aristotle uses "so-called" with "mother wasps" with greater regularity than he does with "king bees." This is probably not significant, though it might mean that he had accepted the term "king bees" for the leaders of the bees more than he had "mother wasps" for the leaders of the wasps (though that is by no means clear). But in light of Aristotle's conclusions regarding the sex of the king bees and of the mother wasps, this difference is not important.

Aristotle is well-aware of the limitations of theory and of the importance of observation.[11] Recall that he writes: "So, this seems to be the way things are concerning the generation of bees, judging from theory and from what are thought to be the facts about them. The facts, however, have not yet been sufficiently grasped; but if they are ever grasped, then we must rely on sense perception more than on theories, and on theories only if what they set forth agrees with what has been observed" (760b27–33). These do not sound like the words of a thinker moved more by ideology and theory than by the observation of facts (untainted by gender bias). Nor does his brief account, in *HA* 8 (9).42, of the anthrenas (αἱ ἀνθρῆναι, perhaps a kind of hornet), which follows his account of wasps in *HA* 8 (9).41. Aristotle says of the anthrenas that "they have leaders like the bees and the wasps" (629a2–3), but that "nothing has been observed yet concerning the copulation of the anthrenas nor where the embryo comes from" (629a22–24).[12]

BEES: DEFENSIVE WEAPONS AND CARE OF OFFSPRING

But scholars suspicious of Aristotle's motives could (and do) point to other parts of his discussion of bees as evidence of prejudice affecting his entomological claims. G. E. R. Lloyd mentions the following passage from *GA* 3.10 (1983, 102): "But it is not reasonable to hold that the worker bees are female and the drones male. For nature gives weapons for defense to no females; but the drones are stingless while the worker-bees have a sting. Nor is the opposite view reasonable, that the worker bees are male and the drones female, for no males are accustomed to doing work for their offspring, but as it is, the worker bees do this" (759b1–7; see 759b27–32).

Lloyd believes this argument involves the application of the following two biased generalizations: (1) females do not possess defensive parts; and (2) males do not share in the care of their offspring.[13] He writes:

> Although some of these generalisations are too sweeping, many obviously have substantial evidence in their support. Common, often large, animals provide most of Aristotle's examples—cattle, deer, the barnyard cock—

11. Regarding what the beekeepers say, see *HA* 8 (9).40.623b19, 22, 31, 624a18, 27, 29, 624b7–11, 625b6, 11–12, 626a1, 10, 626a33–b1, 3, 14, 627a16, 627b6, 12, 16, 19; 8 (9).41.628a7–10, 628b14–30.

12. On anthrenas, see Beavis (1988, 187–92).

13. On the first claim, see *PA* 3.1.661b28–662a6 and *HA* 4.11.538b15–24; on the second, see *HA* 8 (9).1.608b2, and cf. *NE* 8.12.1161b26–27.

and it is to them that the generalisations are particularly applied. Problems arise, however, even in this area, when Aristotle appeals to his general principles to make inferences in doubtful cases. Like the doctrine that males do not, as a general rule, tend their young, the principle that nature does not assign defensive weapons to females is cited in his unfortunate discussion of the sex of bees and is one of the grounds on which he rejects the idea that the worker bees (which have stings) are female. (1983, 102)

Moreover, according to Lloyd these two generalizations contradict what Aristotle says elsewhere. In his discussion of defensive parts, Aristotle says that females either do not possess defensive weapons or, among those that do, their weapons are smaller than those of the males. And as for the claim that males do not help in caring for their young, Lloyd mentions the following exceptions: the glanis, which is a kind of river fish (*HA* 8 [9].37. 621a20–23), and phalangia spiders (*HA* 5.27.555b9–15). (I would add to the list "widower" roosters [*HA* 8 (9).49.631b13–16].)

Is Aristotle ignoring evidence to support his prejudices? Is he guilty of contradictions? A yes to either question would support the view that he engaged in ideological rationalization. That Aristotle uses the emphatic language he does in the above *GA* 3.10 passage ("nature gives weapons for defense to no females. . . ," "no males are accustomed to doing work for their offspring . . .") may be the result of the influence of certain ancient Greek cultural norms. But I don't think this influence goes very deep here (these lines are not characteristic of *GA* 3.10 generally) and see no reason to answer either question in the affirmative. I agree with James Lennox's response to Lloyd:

> As Lloyd sees it, Aristotle takes a theory well-supported in large familiar animals—nature usually does not provide defensive organs to females— and applies it here, reaching the conclusion that worker bees cannot be female. But as the passages quoted by Lloyd . . . show, Aristotle does not see this as a reliable generalization, and at any rate it is one side of a plausibility [εὔλογον] argument which also provides evidence *against* worker bees being *male* (they tend the offspring)—again not certain evidence, for Aristotle allows that males of a few kinds do tend the young. . . . This is surely why Aristotle himself, in a passage Lloyd refers to elsewhere . . . but does not discuss [*GA* 3.10.760b27–33, quoted above], insists that his discussion is all based on λόγος and opinion, and the facts of perception must decide which theory we ultimately adopt. (1985, 350)

In *GA* 3.10, Aristotle says that he reasons first from the facts "peculiar to bees" and then from facts that apply "more generally to all animals" (759a25–27). Given that observation has not sufficiently solved the puzzle of the generation of bees, the best approach, in his view, is to accept tentatively what is true among most animals generally, namely, that males do not tend to their young and that females do not possess defensive weapons. We have every reason to believe that had Aristotle gathered empirical data contradicting these generalizations, he would have revised his position.

MALE INSECTS: SMALLER AND "SEXUALLY PASSIVE"

Leaving bees but sticking to insects—and particularly, insects that generate through copulation—I want to look at another of Aristotle's views that I think supports the claim that in his study of insects he was basically motivated by a desire to observe the facts objectively and not by a desire to rationalize current Greek attitudes. In at least a half dozen passages in the *History of Animals* and the *Generation of Animals,* Aristotle states that, for most insects, the male is smaller than the female and that copulation involves the female penetrating the male. For example: "Insects copulate at the rear, and the smaller (this is the male) mounts the larger. The female inserts, from below, her passage into the male, who is above, and not the male into the female, as in other animals" (*HA* 5.8.541b34–542a3).[14]

These do not sound like the words of a scientist whose views are distorted by his acceptance of common Greek assumptions about the inferiority of females to males and the proper roles of both in generation but, rather, like those of an objective entomologist. This is especially true if Kenneth Dover is right that the ancient Greeks held that an honorable man (even one involved in what was considered a proper homosexual relationship) "never permits penetration of any orifice in his body, and never assimilates himself to a woman by playing a subordinate role in a position of contact" (1989, 103).

* * *

In conclusion, I think it is clear that gender bias did not influence Aristotle's study of insects and, particularly, did not lead him to use the term "kings" to describe the leaders of the bees. In fact, little in his entomology comes close to fulfilling even point 1 of the test for ideological rationaliza-

---

14. See also *HA* 5.19.550b22, 5.28.555b19–22, 5.30.556a25–29; *GA* 1.16.721a11–19, 1.18.723b19–25, 1.21.729b22–25, 2.4.739a18–20.

tion described in the previous chapter (namely, that "the claim does in fact tend to justify the interests of men at the expense of the interests of women"). This should serve as a warning against agreeing too hastily with what certain scholars commenting on Aristotle have concluded is obvious ideological prejudice.

|

THREE

Aristotle's conception of the female's contribution to generation is so widely misunderstood that in this chapter I begin not with what Aristotle says but with what he is often believed to have said. I then turn to what he in fact said and, finally, I examine whether his account of generation is the result of gender bias—as is often claimed—and if so, to what extent.[1]

APOLLO, ARISTOTLE, AND FEMINIST SCHOLARSHIP

In the *Eumenides* (the third play in Aeschylus's *Oresteia* trilogy), Orestes is pursued by the Furies for killing his mother Clytemnestra. Prompted by Apollo, he flees to Athens, where Athena orders a trial by jury to determine his guilt or innocence. At the trial, Apollo speaks these now infamous lines on Orestes' behalf: "She who is called the mother of the child is not a parent, but a nurse of the newly sown embryo [τροφὸς δὲ κύματος νεοσπόρου]. The one who mounts is the parent; but she, like a stranger for a stranger, preserves the young sprout" (lines 658–61).

This passage has given rise to a number of interpretive questions.[2] I am interested in a question indirectly related to this passage, namely, does

1. In this chapter, I do not present a full account of Aristotle's complex and detailed understanding of embryology. I focus on his conception of the female's contribution to generation.

2. For example, what are the roots of this view of generation? Would the audience (in the fifth century B.C.) have taken it seriously or as sophistry aimed at winning a case? Should we evaluate it, in its cultural context, as simply absurd, or as unsurprising given ancient Greek ignorance of the precise nature of generation? Is this a view Aeschylus supports? What, if any, are the ideological implications of such a view? And so on. For some good, brief remarks on this passage, see Lebeck (1988, 42–45) and Sommerstein (1989, 206–8).

Aristotle in any way defend the position of Apollo? Does he view women as mere containers (or as something close to that) in his theory of generation? Judging by the comments of a host of classicists and feminists, one would conclude that the answer is yes—that whatever differences in detail there might be between their views, Aristotle is basically a defender of the position of Aeschylus's Apollo. Are these scholars correct?

Those who put Aristotle and Apollo in the same camp actually fall into two groups: those who defend the "Container Interpretation," according to which Aristotle is, quite simply, a defender of Apollo's position: the female provides a container for the embryo and nourishment to preserve its life and enable it to develop; and those who defend the "Inert Matter Interpretation." According to the latter, Aristotle's position differs from Apollo's in that Aristotle believes females do contribute something more than a container to generation, namely, matter—a passive (and according to some, indeterminate) matter. But given the value Aristotle places on form and activity over matter and passivity, it is claimed, this contribution is so insignificant that in the end Aristotle's position is very close to Apollo's.

Examples of the Container Interpretation can be found in Jean Bethke Elshtain's *Public Man, Private Woman* and in Eva Keuls's *The Reign of the Phallus*. Elshtain writes that "Aristotle buttresses his already strained teleology of female nature with a defective science of biological and reproductive processes." Aristotle, she claims, holds that "the male . . . implants the human form during mating. He deposits within the female a tiny homunculus for which the female serves as a vessel until this creature matures. The female herself provides nothing essential or determinative" (1981, 44).

Keuls, in a section of her book called "The Female as Feedbag," writes: "Aristotle's remarks on sex and procreation reveal the tendentiousness to which Greek biology and medicine had fallen victim. He sought to prove scientifically not only that the male is superior to the female, but also that the female, despite her nurturing of the fetus during pregnancy, has no genetic input into procreation, thus making the father the only real parent" (1993, 145).[3]

Alternatively, the Inert Matter Interpretation finds support from Adriana Cavarero, who, in describing Aristotle's account of the female contribution to generation in her book *In Spite of Plato: A Feminist Reading of An-*

3. Some other examples of this interpretation are Hogan (1984, 171), du Bois (1988, 126), Lebeck (1988, 43), and Rosser (1992, 76).

cient Philosophy, writes that "the material womb contains inert and cold matter" (1995, 72). And Sue Blundell, in *Women in Ancient Greece,* after quoting *Eumenides* 658–61, writes: "This notion of the mother as a mere vessel for carrying the embryo may have occurred in the main on the level of popular belief. Its principle authoritative support is to be found in the work of Aristotle, but there is an important difference between the philosopher's theory and the one expounded by Apollo. According to Aristotle. . . , the female contributes not only space but also matter to the developing embryo. This matter, however, is *entirely passive;* it is the male who supplies the principle of movement and life" (1995, 106, emphasis added).[4]

A careful reading of the *Generation of Animals,* however, reveals that the container and the inert matter interpretations are both inaccurate accounts of Aristotle's embryology.[5]

SEED, SEMEN, AND MENSES

Lesley Ann Dean-Jones, in *Women's Bodies in Classical Greek Science,* relying predominantly on passages from the *Generation of Animals,* writes that

4. Some other examples of this interpretation are Zeitlin (1988, 64–66), Nye (1990, 59), and Tuana (1994, 192).

5. To the information in the *Generation of Animals,* which I discuss in the following pages, one could add some passages from the *History of Animals.* Early in the *History of Animals,* Aristotle writes: "Of those animals in which there belongs generation, one emits into itself, one into another. The one who emits into itself is called 'female,' while the one who emits into another is called 'male'" (*HA* 1.3.489a10–12). Aristotle does not specify what is emitted, but later in the work he seems to imply that it is seed (σπέρμα): "Up to thrice seven years the seeds [σπέρματα] are at first infertile, then they are fertile but the offspring of young men and young women are small and imperfect" (*HA* 9 [7].1.582a16–18). The use of the plural "seeds" (together with the mention of young men and women) suggests, I think, that Aristotle has in mind both male and female seed.

The controversial *HA,* bk. 10, is not a part of the original *History of Animals* but is still worth mentioning. For example: "If indeed the woman too contributes to the seed and to generation, then it is clear that both partners must keep the same pace. So if he finishes quickly while she has hardly done so (for in most things women are slower), this is a hindrance [to generation]" (*HA* 10.5.636b15–19). *History of Animals,* bk. 10, was for many years thought to be inauthentic or, at best, suspect and is still so regarded by some today. (See, e.g., Dean-Jones 1994, 14–15.) But David Balme has argued that *HA,* bk. 10, though not an original part of the *History of Animals,* is nevertheless a genuine (and early) work. (See Balme 1985, 1991, 2, 26–30. For an alternative view of *HA,* bk. 10, consider van der Eijk [1999].)

These *History of Animals* passages seem to suggest that, according to Aristotle, both the male and the female emit seed, and this certainly does not fit the idea that Aristotle accepts the view of generation presented by Aeschylus's Apollo.

one of the most characteristic of Aristotelian doctrines [is] that the woman does not contribute to the conception of the new individual. . . . The theory of female seed, which (in the biological works accepted as genuine) Aristotle argues vehemently *against,* is found nowhere else in the Aristotelian canon and jars with his fundamental dichotomy between form and matter, which in the process of reproduction he equates with male and female respectively. [Aristotle] *did away with the notion of female seed altogether* and asserted that a woman's only contribution to the conception of a foetus was her menses [i.e., καταμήνια] (1994, 14–15, 177, emphasis added).[6]

Because this is a widespread view of Aristotle's conception of the female's contribution to generation, our first order of business is to discover whether—and if so, in what sense—Aristotle believes females as well as males contribute seed to generation. For clarity's sake, I translate the key Greek terms σπέρμα (seed), γονή (semen), and καταμήνια (menses) consistently throughout this chapter.[7]

Early in the *Generation of Animals,* Aristotle writes: "Accepting that animals produced naturally are constituted out of seed, we must not omit to observe how this comes to be produced from the male and from the female" (1.2.716a8–10). It seems that "seed" refers to both the male *and* the female contribution to generation. Balme comments: "At this stage of the argument 'seed' is necessarily vague because Aristotle has not yet analysed for the reader what exactly comes from the female and what from the male" ([1972] 1992, 131).[8] The question is, does Aristotle later revise his view and conclude that the female does not contribute seed to generation?[9]

6. Dean-Jones notes a possible exception at *PA* 4.10.689a11–12, which she calls an "un-Aristotelian remark" (1994, 14n45). (On this passage, see n. 16 below.) I should point out that she rejects the view that Aristotle is in some sense arguing for the position held by Apollo (see 148–53).

On the claim that Aristotle rejected the theory of female seed, see also Lange (1983, 3–6) and Tuana (1994, 192).

7. Balme writes that " 'Seed' (σπέρμα) may refer to (i) seed of a plant; (ii) the male semen (strictly γονή); (iii) the female contribution to generation; (iv) the first stage of the foetus (strictly κύμα, foetus of conception)" ([1972] 1992, 131). I believe he is right, though quite a few scholars (e.g., Dean-Jones and Tuana) seem to disregard this position. In what follows, I hope to lend support to his claim.

8. See also Bolton 1987.

9. At first it appears that terminology will not be a problem, and that Aristotle in fact tells us precisely what he means by such crucial terms as "seed" (σπέρμα) and "semen" (γονή). "That which comes from the generator, in those animals that by nature copulate, is

In the early parts of *GA* book 1, Aristotle clearly uses "seed" to refer to the male contribution to generation (e.g., 1.4.717a29–31, 1.5.717b23–26, 1.13.719b30–33); at places he even uses "seed" and "semen" interchangeably (e.g., 1.6.718a2–14, 1.12.719a35–b4). But the most important parts of the *Generation of Animals* for discovering whether females contribute seed are *GA* 1.17–23, which contain Aristotle's investigation into the nature of the male and female contributions to generation.

In *GA* 1.17, Aristotle raises the issue of the female's contribution: "We must consider this, whether all males [i.e., the male of every kind of animal] emit seed or not all, and if not all, why some do while others do not; and whether the females contribute any seed or not, and if not seed, whether they contribute nothing at all, or whether they contribute something, but not seed. We must further consider . . . what is the nature of the seed and of the fluid called menses in those animals that emit this" (721a32–b6; cf. *GA* 4.1.763b30–33). Shortly thereafter, Aristotle adds: "It is part of the same argument whether both male and female emit seed or only one, and whether it comes from all the body or not from all" (1.17.721b7–10). This line is important, because it will provide part of the context for understanding some of Aristotle's claims about the female's contribution to generation.

The remainder of *GA* 1.17, and much of 1.18, contains the presentation and refutation of the pangenesis theory of generation (i.e., the theory that claims that both male and female contribute seed and that seed is drawn from all parts of the body). At one point, Aristotle seems to support the view that "the female does not emit seed" but is, instead, "a cause of generation in some other way" (724a7–11).[10] On its own, we cannot be clear as to whether this passage rejects the view that the female *contributes* seed or that the female *emits* seed.

---

called semen, that in which the principle of generation is first contained. But seed is that which contains the principles [of generation] from both of the animals which have copulated. . . . Seed and fruit [καρπός] differ by the prior and the posterior, for fruit [is posterior] in that it is out of another, while seed [is prior] in that another is out of it, but both are in fact the same thing" (GA 1.18.724b12–21). But as Balme points out in his comment on this passage, "Aristotle unfortunately does not adhere to these valid and useful distinctions: cf. 728b33 where 'seed' (sperma) stands for all three in turn. This note is probably an insertion, but need not be non-Aristotelian" (Balme [1972] 1992, 145). (See also Peck 1942, 76.) As I will argue, Aristotle comes close to this definition of "seed," with this difference: seed is that which contains the principles of generation from either of the animals that has copulated.

10. I say "seems" because the statement is part of a hypothetical that Aristotle appears to accept.

In *GA* 1.18, Aristotle raises the question, What is seed? He answers that "to be seed means to be by nature the sort of thing out of which naturally constituted things are produced in the first place" (724a17–18). But, he adds, there are different ways in which one thing can be said to come out of another (724a20–21). The two relevant ways here are "out of matter" and/or "out of proximate mover": "The seed is plainly in one of these two classes: it is either as out of matter [ἐξ ὕλης] or as out of proximate mover [ἐκ πρώτου κινήσαντος] that the product comes out of it" (724a35–b1). A few lines later he makes it clear that seed must be matter or mover *or even both* (ἢ καὶ ἄμφω) (724b6).

We learn that residue is surplus nutriment and that seed is a useful residue (724b23–725a21). Although Aristotle often uses "seed" in *GA* 1.18 to refer to the male contribution to generation, he clearly believes that the male and female contributions are both residues and that they are similar (725b31–34, 726a2–6, see also 1.19.727a30–b1).

In *GA* 1.19, Aristotle proceeds to discuss the nature of menses. Since he just covered seed, this implies that, on his view, either menses is not seed or it is a different kind of seed. The chapter opens as follows:

> We must determine what sort of nutriment [male seed] is a residue of, and the same with regard to menses. . . . In this way it will be clear whether [1] the female emits seed like the male [ὥσπερ τὸ ἄρρεν] and what comes to be is one mixture of two seeds, or [2] whether no seed [of any kind or like the male's?] is secreted from the female; and if no seed, whether she contributes [2a] nothing else to generation but only provides a place, or [2b] she contributes something, and if so, how and in what manner. (726a28–b1)

Aristotle will now deal directly with the female contribution to generation. Note that he treats the idea of the female emitting seed (or seed like the male's) with the view that both male and female emit seed, which mingle and become the embryo. I mention this, as I did earlier, because in passages in which Aristotle says the female does not emit seed, we must ask whether he is in fact saying that the female does not emit seed like the male and the two mingle, for that is not the same as denying that the female contributes any kind of seed. (Note also that Aristotle is well aware of the view of Aeschylus's Apollo ["only provides a place"].)[11]

11. In addition, in *GA* 4.1, he refers to, and rejects, the view of "Anaxagoras and other physiologists," who hold, in part, "that the seed comes into being from the male, while the female provides the place for it" (763b31–33).

A bit later in *GA* 1.19, Aristotle says: "Since the semen is a residue of nutriment in its last stage, it will be either blood or the analogous part or something out of these. And since each bodily part is produced out of the blood as it is being concocted and somehow particularized, and since seed (although quite different from blood when it is secreted after concoction) when unconcocted and when forced out by too infrequent sexual indulgence has sometimes come out still bloodlike, it is evident that the seed must be a residue of the nutriment which has become blood" (726b3–10). Aristotle seems to be saying that seed can be concocted and unconcocted and that when it is concocted (i.e., when it is semen), it is (i.e., looks?) quite different from blood, though when it is unconcocted, it is (i.e., it looks like?) blood. In this passage, concocted seed clearly refers to male seed, but it does not rule out the female contribution being seed (though unconcocted seed). This is the position Aristotle is leading up to. "Since the weaker animal must produce residue that is more abundant and less concocted, and being such it must consist of a quantity of bloodlike fluid, and since the weaker is that which has naturally the smaller share of heat, and the female is such . . . , it must follow that the bloodlike secretion produced in the female is a residue too. Such a production is the discharge called menses. Plainly then the menses are a residue and are analogous in females to the semen in males" (1.19.726b30–727a4; see also 727a27–30). Clearly, however different semen and menses are, they are nevertheless similar. He provides further argumentation for this: for example, semen appears in males at the same time of life that menses appears in females; semen disappears in older men at the same time of life that menses disappears in older women (1.19.727a4–10).[12]

Not long after this passage, Aristotle writes that "the female does not contribute seed to generation" (727a27–28) and "menses is a residue just as seed is" (727a30–31). He is clearly using "seed" to refer to "fully concocted seed," that is, to semen. But not a dozen lines later, he says that "the female does not emit the kind of seed that the male emits, and generation is not due to the mixing of both as some hold" (727b6–7). The reason Aristotle here says that the female does not emit seed is that he specifically has in mind the view that holds that both the male and the female *emit* seed and that these seeds mingle to produce the embryo. That is what Aristotle is rejecting, not simply the view that the female contributes seed—though a kind of seed different from the male's—to generation. What is the differ-

---

12. For more arguments showing the similarity between semen and menses, see 1.19.727a10–25.

ence, then, between the male seed and the female seed? I answer this question in greater detail later. But for now, I shall simply point out that the female is different in that she is "not able to concoct seed out of the nutriment in its last stage" (728a18–20).

In *GA* 1.20, Aristotle writes that "menses is seed that is not pure seed but needs working on" (728a26–27). Shortly thereafter he writes that "the female does not emit seed" (728a31–34). He also says that "seed is in the menses" (728b22), and the context of this passage makes it clear that this is equivalent to saying that menses is a residue analogous to semen (cf. 728b21–25 and 1.19.727a4–10).[13] Later in *GA* 1.20, he writes: "The female does not contribute semen to generation, but contributes something, and this is the constitution of menses" (729a20–23; see also 729a30–31).

A consideration of what *GA* book 1 says about the female contribution to generation—and of Aristotle's use therein of σπέρμα (seed), γονή (semen), and καταμήνια (menses)—allows us to come to some preliminary conclusions. First, the Container Interpretation is utterly without basis. It is a ludicrous "reading" of Aristotle—so much so that it leaves one wondering whether its advocates ever read any of the *Generation of Animals*.[14] Second, a consideration of *GA* book 1 gives us some prima facie evidence for being suspicious about the claim of Dean-Jones and others that (in Dean-Jones's words) Aristotle "did away with the notion of female seed altogether" (1994, 177). For there is certainly evidence for the view that Aristotle believes the female contributes some kind of seed (σπέρμα) to generation.

Judging from *GA* book 1, here is how Aristotle uses the key "spermatic" terms: There are two kinds of spermatic residues: semen (γονή) and menses (καταμήνια). Semen is pure, fully concocted seed (σπέρμα); menses is not pure—not fully concocted—seed. This explains why Aristotle sometimes uses "seed" broadly to refer to either or both kinds of spermatic residues, though he often uses "seed" to refer to semen alone.

This terminology (and its loose use) is not confined to *GA* book 1 or to Aristotle's initial discussion of generation. Throughout *GA* book 2,

---

13. Aristotle says "in the menses," because most of the menses is not spermatic, only the most concentrated part. See *GA* 2.4.739a7–13.

14. As one example of the Container Interpretation, I quoted Elshtain, who claims that Aristotle believed the male "deposits within the female a tiny homunculus." Note that not only did Aristotle reject the view that the male deposited a homunculus into the female, in *GA* 1.18 he also rejected Empedocles' theory, which held that the male and the female each contribute half a homunculus, so to speak, to generation.

"semen" and "seed" are used interchangeably.[15] In *GA* 2.3, he says that "the menses is seed but not pure [seed]" (737a28–29); in the following chapter, however, he rejects the idea that the female emits seed (739b16–20). But in *GA* 2.7, spermatic residue (τὸ περίττωμα τὸ σπερματικόν) clearly refers to menses in females and to semen in males (746b26–29).

In *GA* 3.1, discussing oviparous animals, Aristotle writes that the male emits semen (749a15–16), and he uses "seed" to refer to both semen and menses (749b3–9). He also says that "spermatic matter [τὴν ὕλην τὴν σπερματικήν] is present in the female" (750b4–5). Interestingly, he reports in *GA* 3.11 that certain shellfish emit something spermatic (σπερματικῆς), though it should not be considered genuine seed (σπέρμα) (761b31–34). As far as I know, Aristotle never uses such language to describe the female seed.

In *GA* 4.1, he says that the female does not secrete pure residue (765b35–36), and he refers to both male seed and female seed (766b12–14). In *GA* 4.4, he says that "the matter in the female" is "spermatic residue" (771b22–23), and refers to the female contribution to generation as "spermatic matter" (772a2–3). In *GA* 4.5, he writes that "in females, the discharge [κάθαρσις] of menses is the emission of seed [σπέρματος ἔξοδός ἐστιν], for menses is unconcocted seed [σπέρμα ἄπεπτον], as was said earlier" (773b35–774a3). Further, "the voice of both the male and the female change, when [at puberty] *they* begin to produce seed" (*GA* 4.8.776b15–16, emphasis added). However, in the last book of the *Generation of Animals,* Aristotle says that "both [women and children] are incapable of producing spermatic secretion [σπερματικῆς ἐκκρίσεως]" (*GA* 5.3.784a5–6).[16]

Aristotle's use of terminology is certainly loose, but conceptually, what he is saying is coherent: Menses (καταμήνια) is a spermatic residue similar or analogous to semen (γονή). Spermatic residue is seed or has seed in it. Female spermatic residue is generally called menses, though it can also

---

15. For example, see *GA* 2.1.733b16–23, 2.2.735a29–32, 736a13–14, 2.3.736a24–25, 737a7–8, 2.7.747a13–22, 2.8.748a31–35.

16. In an odd passage in *PA* 4.10, Aristotle seems to refer to a part of the female that emits semen (γονή). He writes: "And of the same character too is the menses in females, and that by which they emit semen [τὸν αὐτὸν δὲ τρόπον καὶ ἐν τοῖς θήλεσι τά τε καταμήνια, καὶ ᾗ προΐενται τὴν γονήν]" (689a11–12). To avoid this problem, Düring (1943, 193) suggests that we should read οἱ ἄρρενες (the males) as the subject of προΐενται: "They [the males] emit semen." This is almost certainly the correct way to read this line.

be called seed (σπέρμα); male spermatic residue is sometimes referred to as semen, though it is usually called seed.

Aristotle sometimes uses "seed" in a neutral way to refer to any contribution to generation. As such, it can refer to both semen and menses, though it more often refers to the former. "Seed" and "semen" are often used interchangeably for the male's contribution to generation, and "seed" and "menses" are sometimes used interchangeably for the female's contribution. When Aristotle says that the female does not contribute seed to generation, he must mean that the female does not contribute to generation the kind of seed that the male does—that she contributes unconcocted (i.e., not fully concocted) seed.[17]

Let me clarify of what the male is capable (and the female incapable). In *GA* 2.3, Aristotle writes that "within the seed of everything there is present that which makes the seed to be fertile, the so-called hot. This is not fire or that sort of capability, but the *pneuma* enclosed within the seed and within the foamy part, and more precisely the nature in the *pneuma*" (736b33–37). Male seed, Aristotle held, was a combination of water and *pneuma* (πνεῦμα), the latter being hot air (2.2.736a1). This *pneuma* contains "soul-heat" (θερμότητα ψυχικήν) (3.11.762a20), and it is "by means of *pneuma* that the parts of animals are differentiated" as the embryo develops (2.6.741b37). This is what it means to say that in generation, the male contributes movements and form, or imparts soul to, the matter of the female.[18]

This is the special kind of heat that the female lacks and without which she cannot generate an offspring on her own. This is not to rule out, however, the female contributing heat or movements to generation and being responsible for some concoction. Aristotle says that *pneuma* is not the only heat that can lead to generation; any natural residue has within it some capacity to contribute to generation (2.3.737a2–7). This is why, among

---

17. Balme (1985, 197) writes: "Although in Gen. An. Aristotle frequently repeats that the female contributes no seed, his more detailed arguments there show that this statement refers to seed that is fully comparable with male seed." Albertus Magnus writes that since the menses is simply matter suitable for generation, "it only possesses the name 'seed' equivocally" (*De animalibus* 9.2.3 [Theophrastus from 376B, in Fortenbaugh et al. 1992, their translation]). Compare Lloyd 1983, 95–96, 96n140).

18. For more on Aristotle's conception of the role of *pneuma* in generation, see Peck (1942, app. B) and Balme ([1972] 1992, 160–65). Peck suggests—and he may be right—that the *pneuma* that differentiates the animal parts is not the very same *pneuma* originally contained in the male seed (though it is the same in nature).

quadrupeds that lay eggs, the climate and the heat from the earth complete the concoction of the eggs and, in the case of birds, the heat from the mother who sits her eggs (3.2.753a5–21). Later, we shall see that viviparous females, too, are capable of contributing to concoction.

MALE CONTRIBUTION AS FORM,
FEMALE CONTRIBUTION AS MATTER

Early in the *Generation of Animals,* Aristotle writes that "the male and the female might be considered the chief sources of generation, the male as containing the source of the movement and generation, the female the matter" (1.2.716a4–7). There is a similar passage in *GA* 2.4: "The female always provides the matter, the male provides that which fashions the matter into shape; this, in our view, is the specific characteristic of each of the sexes: that is what it means to be either male or female. . . . The physical part, the body, comes from the female, and the soul from the male, since soul is the essence of a particular body" (738b20–27). In these and many other passages in the *Generation of Animals,* we learn that according to Aristotle, the female provides the matter necessary for generation (the menses), whereas the male provides that which sets, concocts, shapes, forms (i.e., gives form to), ensouls, this matter.[19] In *GA* 2.1, he writes: "Since the source [ἀρχὴ] [of living things] is the male and the female, it must be for the sake of generation that the female and the male exist in those that have them. But the proximate moving cause (in which the definition [λόγος] is present, and the form) is better and more divine in its nature than the matter; and it is better that the superior be separated from the inferior. This is why wherever possible and as far as possible the male is separated from the female" (732a1–7). I take Aristotle to be reasoning in the following way:

1. In generation, there must be the male and the female.
2. One of these must be the moving cause (to which belongs definition and form), and one must contribute the matter.
3. Definition and form are superior to matter (i.e., they are more significant—they most of all say of a thing what it is).
4. Where possible, the superior should be separated from the inferior.

19. See also 1.9.727b31–33, 1.20.729a9–11, 1.21.729a28–31, 730a27, 2.1.732a1–9, 4.1.765b8–15, 766b12–14.

5. The male contributes the definition and form, the female contributes the matter.

6. Therefore, it is better, where possible, for the male and the female to be separate.

This argument raises several questions, but for our purposes, the most significant premise is 5.[20] Why does Aristotle believe that the male contributes the form (which is superior), while the female contributes the matter (which is inferior)?

One reason is found in his account of why generation takes place in the female: "Some matter must be present immediately, already collected, out of which the fetus is constituted in the first place; other matter must continually be added so that what is being gestated may grow. Therefore birth must take place in the female; for the carpenter too is by the timber, the potter by the clay, and in general every act of working upon and proximate movement takes place by the matter, for example building takes place in what is being built" (1.22.730a32–b8). That generation takes place in the female could be used to support Aristotle's claim that the female contributes the matter.

But Aristotle probably found the strongest support for his position in his observation of the facts of generation that were available to him, in combination with the principles of his natural philosophy. According to Aristotle, there are four fundamental powers, which are the causes of the elements: hot, cold, wet, and dry. The four elements are fire (hot and dry), air (hot and wet), earth (cold and dry), and water (cold and wet). At the material level, most changes—and certainly concoction—are owing to heat acting on dry (earthen) or wet compounds, which are relatively cool. (See *Meteorology* 4.1–2, *GC* 2.1–3.) Now Aristotle knew that the female could not generate without the male. (In his language, the female cannot,

20. Premise 4 states that, where possible, the superior should be separated from the inferior. The male and the female are separate in animals but not in plants. The essential difference between plants and animals is that plants do not possess any cognitive abilities, whereas every animal possesses at least some kind of cognition. So, Aristotle reasons, this separation must have something to do with cognition. (See *GA* 1.23.731a24–b8.) But it is still unclear what (cognitive) function separating the male and the female serves. Balme offers the following comment: "The male is superior, and it is better for the superior to be separated from the inferior—presumably because the male can function better as a cognitive animal when not combined with the more material female nature" ([1972] 1992, 153). If correct, Balme's reading would likely give greater force to the claim that Aristotle's argument is—at least in some respects—ideologically motivated.

by herself, fully concoct her seed.) This is fairly obvious. Since he believes generation, like most other changes, involves the heating of a special kind of matter, and since the female cannot generate alone, but can with the male, therefore the male must be the source of greater heat.

Similarly, I take it that his position is based in part on the reasonable assumption that activity, movement, concoction, and fertility are related to heat, whereas less—or a lack of—activity, movement, concoction, and fertility is related to coldness. (See *GA* 1.20.729a20–31, 1.21.729b12–13; *GC* 2.3.) According to Aristotle, the male is warmer than the female; the female's contribution to generation is derived from cooler, less concocted blood.[21] In *GA* 1.19, Aristotle writes that "the weaker animal must produce residue that is more abundant and less concocted, and being such it must consist of a quantity of bloodlike fluid, and . . . the weaker is that which has naturally the smaller share of heat, and the female is such (as previously stated)" (726b30–34).

This reasoning suggests one way in which Aristotle perceives the male as hotter than the female, but this is not his only argument in support of that claim.[22] Here is how I take him to be reasoning in *GA* 4.1.765b6–35:[23]

1. Semen and menses are both residues of blood, and are similar or analogous (this was argued for earlier, as we have seen).
2. All concoction works by means of heat.
3. The female is more abundant in blood than the male in certain parts of the body (this refers, presumably, to menstruation).
4. Semen is less abundant in males than menses is in females, and it is less bloodlike in appearance than menses.

21. See *PA* 2.2.648a9–13, 2.7.653a25–b1; *GA* 1.7.718a20–25, 1.10–11.718b34–38, 1.18. 723a23–26, 1.20.728a18–21, 2.1.733a33–b16, 2.3.736b33–35, 2.4.738a9–16, 2.8.748b31–32, 4.1. 765b6–35, 4.2.766b27–767a8, 4.6.775a4–22. On problems and ambiguities in Aristotle's discussion of male and female blood, see Lloyd (1983, 32–34, 100–101).

22. Balme comments: "That females are colder than males has not been 'previously stated' (726b34), but is a commonplace that Aristotle accepts from tradition" ([1972] 1992, 147). Balme is right that this was a widely held view, but there were some dissenters. As Aristotle writes in *PA* 2.2, it was a topic of debate whether the female's blood was hotter or colder than the males (with Parmenides defending the view that the female's blood is hotter, and Empedocles the opposite; 648a28–32—see also *GA* 4.1.765b17–35). (See Lloyd 1966, 58–59.) Thus I find it doubtful that Aristotle simply accepted the view because it was a commonplace.

23. I restrict myself to the points that concern or lead up to his view that the male is warmer than the female.

5. Therefore, menses is not fully concocted blood, and semen is purer
—that is, more fully concocted—than is menses.
6. Therefore, males are hotter than females.

When Aristotle refers to the male's contribution as superior and the female's as inferior, I think we can assume that in the present context "inferior" and "weaker" refer to what is physically inferior and weaker: smaller, shorter, colder (i.e., lacking in heat), and so on. Now Aristotle may have thought that a general principle about the nature of females (namely, that they are physically inferior) supports his conclusion that females have cooler blood than males and thus cannot fully concoct seed. But he need not have relied on such a deduction, there is no evidence that he did rely on it, and finally, if he had, he would no doubt have claimed that at least he has support for the principle—namely, observations about the relative size, strength, possession of defensive parts, and so forth of females. So, looking ahead, the arguments in support of his view of the different contributions of the male and the female to generation—however flawed— do not rest on simply arbitrary or implausible assumptions.

MALE CONTRIBUTION AS ACTIVE, FEMALE CONTRIBUTION AS PASSIVE

As a corollary to his claim that the female provides the matter, the male that which forms the matter, Aristotle held that the male's contribution is active, whereas the female's is passive. "The female qua female is the patient, while the male qua male is the agent and is that from which comes the beginning of the movement. So that if we take the extremes of each, whereby the one is agent and mover while the other is patient and moved, the one thing being produced is not out of these except in the way that bed is out of carpenter and wood or the sphere out of the wax and the form" (1.21.729b12–18; see also 2.4.740b18–25). Just how "passive" is the matter contributed by the female? Is it anything like the matter purported to be found in Aristotle by those who hold the Inert Matter Interpretation? That is, is the passive matter she contributes inert—does it in no way act (e.g., by having no motions or movements of its own) and/or does it in no way have a nature of its own (because it is indeterminate)? On this view, it seems the female's contribution would have to be something like an indeterminate "prime" matter.

There is a passage that might be thought to support this interpretation of Aristotle: "If the male exists as active and causing movement and the female as passive, then the female will contribute to the male's semen not semen but matter. And this is clearly her contribution, for the nature of the menses is in accordance with the prime matter [τὴν πρώτην ὕλην]" (GA 1.20.729a28–33). What does Aristotle mean by "prime matter" here? If he has in mind anything like the traditional conception of prime matter—an indeterminate substratum out of which the four elements arise—then it seems the female's contribution is extremely passive and inert indeed.

Some scholars have raised strong doubts about there being any such conception of prime matter in Aristotle's thought.[24] But putting these doubts aside, the fact that the menses is a certain kind of residue of blood—bearing potentiality for a specific kind of offspring—alone suggests that it is not prime matter in this indeterminate sense. David Balme is correct in characterizing the menses as "proximate matter"—prime matter in relation to the fetus.[25] This becomes especially clear in light of a passage in GA 2.6, which makes further use of the carpenter analogy:

> This heat [from the male seed], to produce flesh and bone, does not work on some casual matter in some casual place at some casual time; matter, place and time must be those ordained by nature: that which is potentially will not be brought into being by a motive agent that lacks the appropriate actuality; so equally, that which possesses the actuality will not produce the article out of any casual matter. No more could a carpenter produce a chest out of anything by wood; and equally, without the carpenter no chest will be produced out of the wood. (743a21–26)

The male and female contributions are treated here as equal and mutually necessary principles of generation—as specific kinds of heat and matter, without which the specific animal could not be formed. In fact, Aristotle says on numerous occasions that the menses is the animal and its parts in potentiality. For example, in GA 3.11, he writes that menses is "a residue which potentially is such as the parent is from which it came, and which is perfected into an animal by the principle from the male imparting movement to it" (762b2–6).[26]

But in what sense, then, is the male contribution active and the female

---

24. See, e.g., the appendix in Charlton ([1970] 1992, 129–45) titled "Did Aristotle Believe in Prime Matter?"

25. See Balme [1972] 1992, 152; 1985, 197.

26. See also 1.19.726b15–24, 2.3.737a22–24, 2.4.740a1–9, 740b18–20, 2.5.741b7–8.

passive? An analogy Aristotle sees between the semen acting on menses, and fig juice or rennet acting on milk, is illuminating: "The male provides both the form and the source of movement, while the female provides the body, i.e., the matter. Just as in the curdling of milk, the milk is the body, while the fig juice or rennet contains the principle that sets it, so is what comes from the male when it is partitioned in the female" (1.20.729a9–14). And this is a pretty close analogy, Aristotle claims, because "the nature of milk and the nature of menses are the same," and so, therefore, is the action of semen on menses the same as fig juice or rennet on milk (2.4. 739b20–27; see also 4.4.771b21–27).[27]

The male seed provides or contains the form and the movements that set or "curdle" the material contribution from the female. The female cannot alone fully concoct or form her seed into an embryo or produce a fully concocted seed. In this sense, she contributes matter alone.[28] And in this sense, the female contribution is passive: the male contribution does the "curdling" while the female contributes what is "curdled." (Recall that in the *Generation of Animals,* Aristotle claims that females are passive only with respect to their contribution to generation. See *GA* 1.21.729b12–18, 2.4.740b18–25.)

SOULS AND MARVELOUS AUTOMATA

To further understand just what the female does (and does not) contribute to generation, let us look briefly at the formation of soul in the embryo.

According to Aristotle, seeds (male and female) and the fetus (at the beginning) possess the nutritive soul (ἡ θρεπτικὴ ψυχή) potentially. When the fetus develops to the point that it can draw in its own food, then it is living like a plant and actually possesses nutritive soul. (See *GA* 2.1.734b22–735a19, 2.3.736b8–13, 737a16–18.) It is clear throughout *GA* 2.3 (and in his account of wind eggs, which I discuss below) that Aristotle regards menses as the source (at least in part) of the nutritive soul of the offspring. What is the female not responsible for? "The menses is seed but not pure [seed], for it lacks one thing only, the source of the soul" (737a28–30)—and by this, Aristotle means the source of sentient soul (ἡ αἰσθητικὴ ψυχή). To become an animal requires the male contribution, for the

---

27. On the nature of milk, and its similarity to menses, see *GA* 4.8.

28. Note that the female contributes all of the matter to generation. None of the matter of the male's seed remains as part of the fetus. See *GA* 1.21.729b18–730a23, 2.3.737a7–16, 2.8.748b32–33.

male produces sentient soul, thereby completing generation (2.5.741a6–16, 741a26–29).[29]

Generation of Animals 2.1 describes part of the process:

> The seed, and the movement and source that it contains, are such that as the movement ceases each part is produced having soul. For it is not face nor flesh unless it has soul: after their death it will be equivocal to say that the one is a face and the other flesh, as it would be if they were made of stone or wood. . . . Now heat and cold would make them [i.e., the various parts] hard and soft and tough and brittle, with all other such affections that belong to the parts containing soul, but would not go so far as giving them the definition in virtue of which the one is now flesh and the other bone: that is due to the movement derived from the generator, which is actually what the thing out of which the product comes is potentially. (734b22–735a4)

The male contribution is responsible for shaping the matter—for actualizing its specific potential—such that it takes on the parts that make sentience possible: not only the parts that directly correspond to the senses (eyes, ears, nose, tongue, skin) but every part that involves the senses. A hand, for example, that does not possess the capacity to feel is not really a hand. As a result of the male's contribution, the embryo (at a certain point) is capable of sentience as well as nutrition and growth.

Should anyone conclude from this that the female's contribution is inert or passive in some significant way—in a way that implies that the female contribution is insignificant—consider Aristotle's analogy between menses and automata. Here are two passages:

> It is possible for this to move this, and this, this, and for it to be like the marvelous automata. For their parts stand there containing somehow a potentiality when they are at rest; and when something outside has moved the first of them, immediately the next one becomes actualized. (2.1.734b9–13)

> As the parts of the animal to be formed are present potentially in the matter, once the principle of movement has been supplied, one thing follows

---

29. To become a human animal requires the acquisition of the rational soul (mind or reason [νοῦς]). The female is not the source of this part of the soul. Is the male? In *GA* 2.3, Aristotle says that at what point, how, and from where a human embryo acquires reason are difficult questions to answer (736b5–8).

on after another without interruption, just as it does in the marvelous automata. (2.5.741b7–9).[30]

However much this analogy leaves unexplained in details, it confirms that menses is not some highly unspecified matter to be made into clay and molded by the male contribution. Rather, the menses is in fact a highly specific set of potential movements—which need to be activated or triggered by the male contribution for generation to take place or be completed.

WIND EGGS

For further evidence that the female's contribution is "rich" rather than "inert," let us turn to GA 2.5, which is devoted to solving the puzzle of why the female needs the male to generate. Plants, Aristotle says, need no separation of the sexes in order to generate because they possess the nutritive soul alone; they are not sentient beings. But since the sentient soul comes from the male in those animals where male and female are separate, the female is unable to generate an animal by itself. (If the female could generate without the male, the male would have no purpose; but, Aristotle says, "nature does nothing in vain" [741b2–5]. I shall have more to say later on why he holds that male and female are separate in many animals.) He continues:

> Still, that the puzzle we have stated is reasonable is evident from the case of those birds which lay wind eggs [τὰ ὑπηνέμια], because *up to a certain point the female is able to generate.* But there is a puzzle here too: In what sense are we to say that these eggs are alive? We cannot say that they are alive in the same sense as fertile eggs, for in that case an actual ensouled [ἔμψυχον] being would hatch out from them; *nor are they like wood and stone* [eggs]. For these [wind] eggs go bad just as fertile ones do, and this seems to indicate that to start with they were in some sense alive. So it is clear that they possess some soul potentially. What sort, then? Of course, it must be the lowest, and this is nutritive [soul]. For this is present in all animals and plants alike. Why then does it [the nutritive soul] fail to bring to completion the parts and the animal? Because they must possess sentient soul, since the parts of animals are not like those of a plant. This is

30. Compare *De motu animalium* 7.701b2–3: "The movement of animals is like that of automata, which are set moving when a small movement occurs: the cables are released and the pegs strike against one another" (trans. from Nussbaum 1985, slightly rev.).

why the female needs the partnership of [or sexual intercourse with] the male [τῆς τοῦ ἄρρενος κοινωνίας], for the male is separated [from the female] in such animals.[31] This is exactly what happens, for the wind eggs become fertile if the male treads [the female] within a certain period. (741a16–32)[32]

We learn from GA 2.5 that Aristotle took observation quite seriously (even in a science where so much is hidden from observation) and that what the female contributes to generation is emphatically not inert, indeterminate matter (like wood or stone). The female's contribution is responsible for some (but not all) of the concoction involved in generation. As we have seen, in GA 2.5 Aristotle also tells us that the parts of the specific animal in question are present potentially in this matter—that is, the female's contribution cannot serve as the matter for any other kind of animal. With the male contribution, Aristotle says, this matter becomes in actuality what it was potentially.

In GA 1.21, Aristotle writes that "in some animals, for example birds, nature can generate up to a point; for these do constitute, but the products—the so-called wind eggs—are imperfect [or incomplete, ἀτελῆ]" (730a30–32). Does this mean that what Aristotle says about wind eggs in GA 2.5 applies not to all females but, merely, to some female birds? No. First, he mentions some animals besides birds, the females of which are capable of producing something like a wind egg: some kinds of fish (GA 1.21.730a18, 2.5.741a32–b2, 3.1.750b8–9, 750b26–32, 3.5.756a15–20) and perhaps some kinds of grasshoppers (HA 10.6.637b16–18)—and women, since the *mola uteri* or uterine mole is, he says, similar to the wind egg. (On uterine moles, see GA 4.7 and HA 10.7.)[33] The uterine mole, a rare occurrence, is, Aristotle says, a fleshy mass not unlike uncooked or underdone meat; on his view, it is the result of an excess of menses, which the woman is able to set but not concoct fully. He says that "in its nature it is neither a finished product nor something wholly alien" (GA 4.7.776a5–6).[34]

But more important, whether a certain kind of bird produces wind eggs does not seem to depend on the nature of its particular menses. Wind eggs are produced "because although spermatic matter is present in the

31. According to LSJ, one meaning of κοινωνία is communion, association, partnership; another is sexual intercourse.

32. See also GA 1.21.729b33–730a32, 2.3.737a30–34, 3.1.750b3–751b31.

33. On HA, bk. 10, see n. 5 above, this chapter.

34. Compare Aristotle's discussion of wind eggs and especially the uterine mole with his account of "monsters" at GA 4.3.769b10–13.

female, among birds no discharge of menses takes place, as it does with blooded viviparous animals" (*GA* 3.1.750b4–6). Further, even among birds, wind eggs are produced only among those kinds for which there is enough residue, because menses and feathers both are formed out of residue, and nature, Aristotle argues, cannot produce a large supply of residue for both menses and feathers. Thus, wind eggs "occur in birds which are neither good fliers nor crook-taloned" (see *GA* 3.1. 749a34–b16, 750b19–21).

THE FEMALE'S CONTRIBUTION TO FAMILY RESEMBLANCE

For further evidence that the female's contribution is not inert matter, I turn to *GA* 4.3, a dark chapter containing Aristotle's account of family resemblance. Here, in brief, are what I understand to be the essential points of Aristotle's theory. Offspring will either take after parents, earlier ancestors, or any human; or (if there is a deviation from type) it will be a monstrosity. Males take after their fathers more, Aristotle believes, and females take after their mothers more. In a sense, he says, the female is already a deviation, though a necessary one—necessary because such a deviation is needed for the perpetuation of the species and because it is possible for the movements of the male's seed sometimes (roughly 50 percent of the time) not to overpower those of the female's.

The process of generation involves both male and female "movements." If the male's movements achieve mastery over the female's in respect to the characteristic of gender, then the offspring is male. If not, it is female.[35] ("The reason why that which is acted on departs from type and does not get mastered is either (*a*) deficient potency in the concocting and motive agent, or (*b*) the bulk and coldness of that which is being concocted and articulated" [*GA* 4.3.768b25–27].) As for other characteristics, if the male's movements achieve mastery, the characteristic will resemble that of his father or of one of his father's ancestors; if not, the characteristic will resemble that of his mother or of one of her ancestors. If the male's movements achieve mastery but relapse, then the characteristic shifts from that of the father to that of the paternal grandfather, say; but if they do not achieve mastery, but the female's movements relapse, then the characteristic shifts from that of the mother to that of the maternal grandmother, say.

Take a nose, for example. If the male's movements master the female's sufficiently, then the offspring will have a nose like its father's. If the male's

35. Note that the sexual parts are not present in the seed. See *GA* 1.18.723a23–b3.

movements master the female's but not sufficiently, there is a relapse, and the nose resembles, for example, the paternal grandfather's. If the male's movements fail to master the female's, then the nose will resemble either the mother's or, if there is a relapse, the maternal grandmother's, for example.[36]

The two passages from *GA* 4.3 that follow illustrate that the female makes a significant contribution to family resemblance—and thus to generation.

> Some of the movements are present in actuality, others in potentiality: in actuality, those of the male parent and those of the universals (e.g., of human being and of animal), while in potentiality, those of the female and those of the ancestors. (768a11–14)

> The reason why the movements relapse is that the agent also gets acted upon by what it acts upon, e.g., that which cuts is blunted by what is cut, and that which heats is cooled by what is heated, and generally, any mover, except for the Prime Mover, is itself moved by a certain movement in return. (768b15–19)

What precisely Aristotle is saying in *GA* 4.3 is difficult to determine. I here briefly mention three attempts to make sense of the chapter. According to Balme, the *Generation of Animals* shows that Aristotle did think that the female makes a formal contribution to generation: "The male contributes the primary formal influence, while the female contribution is primarily material plus a secondary formal influence" (1987, 292).[37] Accord-

---

36. Dean-Jones quite correctly comments that "Aristotle does not address the issue of how a child could resemble his paternal grandmother or his maternal grandfather, but it must involve a combination of relapse and mastery" (1994, 197). (See also Cooper 1990, 73.)

37. See also Balme 1990, 49–54. Compare Albertus Magnus, *De animalibus* 3.2.8 (= Theophrastus fr. 376A Fortenbaugh et al.). He writes:

> The earliest followers of Aristotle, like Theophrastus and Porphyry, distinguished between the informed power and the formative power, saying that the informed power, or putting it better the informable power, is that in which the form is formed, and is in the matter. The form however possesses in itself the formative, or forming power; and they assigned the formative power to the seed of the male, but the informed power they gave to the seed of the female. Each (power) indeed possesses form, but one (possesses a form that is) determinate and acts by its own kind, the other however gives nothing at all to the matter except this, that what is formed can come to be from (the matter) by a power that is ordered and inchoate. (Fortenbaugh et al. 1992, translation)

ing to John Cooper (1990), there are movements in both male and female seeds, and the female contribution plays an important part in generation. Nevertheless, the male's movements alone have an active, formative role. The movements described in the first passage above are all contained in the male seed: the male's movements actually, the female's potentially. The female contributes the matter to generation, and the movements from this matter come into play only when activated by the movements from the male. Finally, Montgomery Furth (1988) claims that there is a tension between Aristotle's general conception of male and female contributions to generation, on the one hand, and what he says about the determination of sex and family resemblance in *GA* 4.1–3, on the other. According to his interpretation, in the earlier books the female contribution is held to be passive, but in *GA* book 4 we find, surprisingly, that the female does contribute movements and thus exerts an active, formative influence.[38]

I cannot here settle the issue of how best to read *GA* 4.3. I tend to think Balme is right, however, for I do not think Cooper's reading can explain the passages on wind eggs, and I think the passages on wind eggs and on automata, among others, show that there is no real tension among the different parts of the *Generation of Animals*. That is, Aristotle held that there were movements in the female's contribution to generation throughout. In any case, *GA* 4.3 and the rest of the *Generation of Animals* (e.g., 1.17–20 and, esp., 2.5) are at the very least consistent in this respect: they both show that according to Aristotle the female does not merely contribute inert matter to generation.

Further, no matter how one takes the female contribution in *GA* 4.3, it cannot plausibly be described as inert. Even if the female's potential movements exist in the male's seed and it is the male's movements that do all the work (as Cooper argues), it remains true that it is the particular nature of this particular female's menses that determines, at least indirectly, what species the offspring is, whether it will be male or female, and, for example, whether it will have its mother's nose. This particular menses does exert an influence on the seed from the male. For Aristotle cannot be saying that when the movements from the father's seed work on the matter from the mother, these movements just happen, coincidentally, to fashion the matter such that the result resembles (in some respects) the mother or her ancestors.

38. Furth 1988, 129–45. See also Dean Jones (1994, 193–95) and Coles (1995).

THE FEMALE'S CONTRIBUTION TO GENERATION:
AN OVERVIEW

The Container Interpretation is simply absurd, and we have extremely good reasons to reject the Inert Matter Interpretation as well. According to Aeschylus's Apollo, the female contributes nothing but space (and nutrition). The male contributes the matter that will make up the fetus, and he determines the offspring's species, gender, and every feature it will possess. If Aristotle's view—that the female contributes the matter alone—is properly or in effect a defense of Apollo's position, then I take it that Aristotle would have to be saying that the female contributes the container and the matter and that the male determines everything else: species, gender, and every feature the offspring will come to possess. This is the only sense I can give to the female's contribution on the Inert Matter Interpretation. But clearly, this does not correspond to Aristotle's conception of the female contribution.

In summary, it is clear that the female contributes something to generation besides simply the container; and what the female contributes —menses—is in some sense seed. According to Aristotle, menses, like semen, is a useful residue (derived from blood or its analogue)—fully concocted in the case of semen, not fully concocted in case of menses (though the female is capable of some concoction). The female provides the matter—all the matter—that the soul heat from the male shapes and provides with form. Menses is in a sense passive, but in no sense is it totally inactive or indeterminate matter. It possesses a specific nature with motions of its own, and it is, potentially, the animal and its parts.

Menses provides, at least in part, nutritive soul to the offspring and also contributes to its gender and appearance. In addition, in passages I have not discussed, Aristotle makes it clear that the female contribution to generation is, in part, responsible for the number of offspring and the size of the offspring.[39]

---

39. On the number of offspring, see *GA* 1.20.729a1–3, 729a16–20, 4.4.769b36–770a7, 772a17–22, 772a30–37, 4.5.773b11–12; on the size of the offspring, see 4.4.771b14–772a12. For a further example supporting the claim that menses exerts an influence in generation, consider this passage from *GA* 2.4: "When a male and a female of different kinds copulate (which happens in the case of animals whose periods are equal and whose times of gestation run close, and which do not differ widely in physical size), the first generation, so far as resemblance goes, takes equally after both parents (e.g., the offspring of fox and dog, and of partridge and common fowl). But as time goes on and successive generations are produced, the offspring

Given all of this, I conclude that the Inert Matter Interpretation is little better than the Container Interpretation and that both should be rejected.

EMBRYOLOGY AND IDEOLOGY

I have shown not only that Aristotle's position is distinct from that of Apollo but that it in fact represents a (fairly explicit) rejection of Apollo's account of generation. So, Aristotle is often saddled with a view of the female's contribution to generation that, it turns out, he did not in fact hold. But can we thus dismiss the charge—often made by the same mistaken interpreters of his biology—that even his actual views on this issue were not the result of honest (though mistaken) science but, rather, of ideological rationalization? I begin with the first point of the test for ideological rationalization—in the present case, whether or to what extent Aristotle's conception of the female contribution to generation tends to justify the interests of men at the expense of those of women.

Jonathan Barnes, in his review of Lloyd (1983), writes:

> Lloyd refers allusively to the "social and political implications" of the view [of Aeschylus's Apollo on generation]. He presumably takes it to imply that matricide is less heinous than patricide, that women do not have full parental rights over their children, that their proper role in the family and in society is a humble one, that they should play no part in the official life of the state, and so on. I cannot for the life of me see why anyone should discern such implications in the theory. The theory does imply, what is true, that the male and the female roles in reproduction are different from each other. It does not, so far as I can see, suggest that the mother, being the seedbed and nursery, somehow plays a subsidiary or unimportant or passive role in the production of offspring. On the contrary, the protection and nutrition of the embryo are evidently indispensable to its well-being. . . . Of course, the Aeschylean view can be twisted to serve an ideological end. But so can any theory. The view itself has no ideological implications. (1984a, 9)

I submit that the same can be said—and with greater confidence—about any ideological implications claimed to be found in Aristotle's account of

---

finish up by taking after the female as regards their bodily form, just as seeds are introduced into a strange locality" (738b27–35). This fact, as Aristotle sees it, can best be explained in terms of the menses exerting a greater influence than the semen in these cases.

generation. Nevertheless, I will also inquire into point 2 of the test—which amounts to a question of how good Aristotle's arguments are—as this might reveal some possibly ideologically loaded premises in Aristotle's defense of his conception of generation.

To consider whether Aristotle was guilty of ideological rationalization, it helps to ask what positions someone working in biology at his time— that is, without a microscope and other discoveries of modern biology— could have come up with about the male and the female contributions to generation. (I have purposely included positions that some scholars have [mistakenly] attributed to Aristotle.) Here are seven possibilities (employing some of Aristotle's terminology):

1. The male contributes everything, the female nothing (but the container [the position of Aeschylus's Apollo]).
2. The female contributes everything, the male nothing (having no role in generation).
3. The male alone contributes seed (and thus form), the female contributes inert matter.
4. The female alone contributes seed (and thus form), the male contributes inert matter.
5. The male and female both contribute seed, but they are different in that the male contributes form, whereas the female contributes "rich" matter (e.g., not fully concocted blood [the position of Aristotle]).
6. The male and female both contribute seed, but they are different in that the female contributes form, whereas the male contributes "rich" matter (e.g., not fully concocted blood);
7. The male and the female both contribute seed (or more generally, they both contribute roughly equal parts), which intermingle to form a new individual (this includes the "pangenesis" theory, and the position of Empedocles).

Of the three of these that favor the male (and thus would have the highest likelihood of being ideologically suspect)—1, 3, and 5—Aristotle rejects positions 1 and 3, the two worst offenders: the two that feminist scholarship often attributes to him and claims puts him in the same camp with Aeschylus's Apollo. Further, Aristotle can rule out position 2 as obviously incorrect; and for reasons given earlier—for example, involving the warmer blood of the male—Aristotle must clearly reject number 4 as well.

Skipping ahead, Aristotle provides argumentation—none of it ideologically motivated, so far as I can tell—for rejecting at least some versions of number 7: the "pangenesis" theory, a view attributed to Hippocrates and to Democritus, according to which both the male and the female contribute seed drawn from all of the body, and, the position of Empedocles, according to which both the male and the female contribute a "tally" (σύμ-βολον), neither of which is a whole, but that both together go to make up the new, whole animal. (See *GA* 1.17–18 and 4.1.764b3–20.)[40]

We are left with positions 5 and 6. For a number of reasons discussed above—the observation that the male and the female are both necessary for generation, combined with principles of Aristotle's natural philosophy; why the male and the female sources of generation are separate; that generation takes place in the female; why male blood is warmer than female blood—Aristotle chose number 5. As I said earlier, his arguments—however mistaken in their conclusions—are neither based on arbitrary or implausible assumptions nor so lacking in merit as to be ideologically suspect.

In chapter 1, I said that Lloyd made a useful distinction when he wrote: "It is . . . clear that the value-laden-ness, including at times the ideological slant, of much of [Aristotle's] work in the life sciences, so far from being fortuitous, or a mere residue from traditional assumptions, corresponds to one of the primary motivations of the Aristotelian enterprise" (1983, 215). Using this language, I would say that Aristotle's conception of the female's contribution to generation is certainly not the result of any primary ideological motivation. He was not, as Eva Keuls claims he was, "one of the fiercest misogynists of all times, obsessed with the need to prove that women played no genetic part in reproduction" (1993, 405). Further, I see little evidence for any "ideological slant"—even as "a mere residue from traditional assumptions."

40. Charles Segal writes that σύμβολον is "a word usually translated as 'clue.' But the word also means a 'tally,' one of two parts of a token that fit together to prove one's rightful place. . . . The word *symbolon* also has another meaning, namely, the 'token' left with a child exposed at birth to establish later proof of his identity" (2001, 65–66).

On the Hippocratic theory, which holds that both the male and the female contribute seed to generation, see Lloyd (1983, 89–94) and Dean-Jones (1994, 153–76).

FOUR

EUNUCHS AND WOMEN

In the *Generation of Animals,* in what is perhaps the most notorious line in his corpus, Aristotle writes that "the female is as it were [ὥσπερ] a mutilated [πεπηρωμένον] male" (2.3.737a27–28).[1] Some scholars believe this line speaks volumes about Aristotle's animus against women. Mary-anne Cline Horowitz describes it as a "devastating catchphrase" (1976, 203), and Eva Keuls sees it as evidence of Aristotle's misogyny (1993, 145).[2] But does the line in fact show that Aristotle was guilty of ideological rationalization?

THE QUALIFIED NATURE OF THIS "MUTILATION"

Allan Gotthelf has shown that when Aristotle describes the female as a mutilated male, he is making a very qualified claim:

> Dwarfs and so on (including, alas, females, whose femaleness we should view ὥσπερ ἀναπηρίαν [*GA* iv 6.775a15–16]) are defined of course relative to the normal (male) members of their kinds. The seal is a (sort of)

1. Elsewhere Aristotle writes that "we should consider the female as being as it were [ὥσπερ] a natural mutilation [ἀναπηρίαν . . . φυσικήν]" (*GA* 4.6.775a15–16). See also *GA* 4.3.767a36–b13. Πηρόω—the root of both πεπηρωμένον and ἀναπηρίαν—means "maim" or "mutilate" (LSJ); and, at least in Aristotle, words related to πηρόω can refer to deformities, i.e., animals "mutilated" from birth (see Gotthelf 1985, 39). Note that in *GA* 1.20, Aristotle says that "a woman is as it were [ὥσπερ] an infertile male [ἄρρεν ἄγονον]" (728a17–18). See Freeland 1994, 172–75.

2. It is devastating, Horowitz claims, because on her view it was "transmitted into biological, obstetrical, and theological tracts and continues to have authoritative influence through St. Thomas Aquinas' *Summa Theologiae*" (1976, 184–85).

deformed *quadruped*. Interestingly, in speaking of kinds that seem to defy classification into wider groups because they have several features, but not all, of each of two such groups (*PA* iv 13—our classic "borderline cases"), Aristotle explains that seals "dualize" [ἐπαμφοτερίζειν]: Professor Balme has suggested "tend in both directions") with respect to being land- and water-animals, and that their hind feet can be considered completely fishlike (697b1–7)—so they are not really quadrupeds. Yet, if we consider them ὥσπερ [as it were] quadrupeds, as we need not but can, they do not do a very good job at it. . . .

Pace anthropologizing interpretations, then, the biological point is that we have organs that cannot perform (as well) the functions they are most-suited for and have developed for. . . , by the standards of the performance of the versions of that organ in the other members of that wider kind. Where the organs perform another function sufficiently well, as the fin-like hind feet do in seals (697b4–6), Aristotle will say, it seems, that they are only ὥσπερ deformed. The female, who has a natural and necessary function, which she performs very well, has her 'deformity' doubly qualified (and perhaps triply, if ἀναπηρία is weaker than πήρωμα—but LSJ is no help towards deciding this). (1985, 39–40)

Aristotle, in calling the female "as it were" a mutilated male, is not saying that she is literally mutilated or deformed; nor is he saying that females are deformed with respect to how they perform their functions. A female's function—for instance, in generation, she provides a certain kind of seed, which is the matter for generation—is performed exactly as it should be, in a way "dictated" by nature, so to speak. But in a sense—for instance, when her contribution to generation is compared to the male's—the female is as it were deformed or imperfect. Unlike the male, Aristotle believes, she cannot fully or completely concoct the matter for generation. (In the same way, from this perspective, a seal is "perfect" with respect to its nature and function; but when compared to normal quadrupeds, it is as it were a deformity or mutilation, i.e., its legs do not function the way a normal quadruped's do.)

At the very least, this passage is not as bad as it perhaps sounds at first. Aristotle does not simply or literally say that females are mutilated males. Nevertheless, even with the more nuanced understanding of the passage provided by Gotthelf, the fact that Aristotle claims that females are as it were deformed when compared to males (who are the standard for what is normal here) might reasonably be thought to have a strong ideological flavor. So we must investigate this passage more fully.

GENERATION OF ANIMALS 2.3.737A24–28

To determine more completely whether or to what extent Aristotle was guilty of ideological rationalization in concluding that "the female is as it were a mutilated male," we must set the context for this claim. What scientific or philosophic problems was Aristotle attempting to resolve? Here is the infamous line in its broader context: "[Menses] even contains potentially the sort of parts whereby there is a difference between male and female. For just as the offspring of mutilated [i.e., deformed] animals [πεπηρωμένων] are sometimes mutilated [πεπηρωμένα] and sometimes not, so that of a female is sometimes female and sometimes not, but male. For the female is as it were a mutilated [πεπηρωμένον] male" (*GA* 2.3.737a24–28).[3] It is in the context of two related investigations that Aristotle chose to view females as analogous to mutilated males.

1. *What determines whether the fetus becomes a male or a female.* As we saw in the previous chapter, Aristotle did not believe that animal generation involves the transmission to the womb of an already formed mini-male or mini-female. The same seed from the father can become either a male or a female. So in attempting to account for the generation of animals, he had to explain the process by which the fetus—a product of seed from the male and seed from the female—becomes a male or a female.

2. *The physical differences between males and females.* This issue is related to inquiry 1 and concerns these questions: Why does a fetus become a male or a female—that is, an animal with the gender specific parts and physical characteristics that it has? Why is it that males and females come to differ not only in genitalia but also in size, shape, voice, ability to go bald, softness of skin, and so on?

I hope to demonstrate that Aristotle concluded, for reasons having little or nothing to do with ideology, that maintaining an analogy between females and mutilated males—between women and eunuchs—had a great deal of explanatory power.

ARISTOTLE'S EXPOSURE TO EUNUCHS AND CASTRATION

The first point to make in support of my hypothesis is that during Aristotle's lifetime he would have had much more exposure to the phenome-

---

3. The passage continues: "And the menses are seed but not pure [seed]." Aristotle's conception of menses was dealt with in the previous chapter and will not concern us here.

non of castration generally—and in particular, castration of boys to make eunuchs—than does the modern scientist.[4] This is important, for the use of a eunuch analogy, or a metaphor of castration, by a twentieth-century thinker might be ideologically loaded in a way that it would not necessarily be for a Greek of the fourth century B.C.

Eunuchs were a regular part of life for Asians—Persians, Medes, Lydians, Babylonians, Assyrians—and Aristotle would have been well aware of this aspect of their cultures. (Greek cities in general had a great deal of contact with and knowledge of "Asians," as did Aristotle's Macedonia, which was, for example, occupied by the Persians from 512 to 479 B.C.) Herodotus reveals just how well (and horribly) the Greeks knew about the oriental practice of castrating boys. He writes that Periander, despot of Corinth (in the sixth century), sent three hundred sons from the chief men of Corcyra to King Alyatander of Lydia for castration as eunuchs (3.48–49). Early in the fifth century, he tells us, the Persians gave the following ultimatum to the Ionian Greeks: remain allies with Persia or we will castrate your boys and carry off your girls to Bactia (6.9). Herodotus also reports that the Persians under Xerxes took eunuchs with them in their campaign against Greece (7.187).[5] In his *Cyropaedia,* Xenophon describes Cyrus's reasons for choosing eunuchs for his bodyguard and includes Cyrus's inference about the nature of eunuchs from what he knew about castrated animals (7.5.57–65). Aristophanes includes eunuchs among the Persian envoy in the *Acharnians* (117, 121); and in the *Laws,* Plato mentions the use of eunuchs in Persia (695a–b).[6]

---

4. Aristotle, after leaving Plato's Academy, spent some time on Assos in the company of the local leader, Hermeias. In a strange passage in his *Geography,* Strabo writes: "Here [in Assos] Aristotle tarried, because of his relationship by marriage with the tyrant Hermeias. Hermeias was a eunuch, the slave of a certain banker; and on his arrival at Athens he became a pupil of both Plato and Aristotle. On his return he shared the tyranny with his master, who had already laid hold of the districts of Atarneus and Assos; and then Hermeias succeeded him and sent for both Aristotle and Xenocrates and took care of them; and he also married his brother's daughter to Aristotle" (13.1.57; translation from Jones 1929). This passage strains belief (one can imagine a tabloid headline describing Hermeias's success: Banker's Slave, Eunuch, Succeeds Master as Local Tyrant), so I have placed it in a note. However, if Strabo's account is accurate about Hermeias being a eunuch, then Aristotle would have had a rather close association with a eunuch and, thus, the opportunity to observe closely his overall physical attributes.

5. See also Herodotus 1.117, 3.4, 77–78, 92, 130, 4.43, 6.32, 8.104–106; Athenaeus 514d; Diodorus Siculus 17.66.4–5.

6. In Plato's *Protagoras,* Protagoras's doorman is a eunuch (314c–d).

One work in the Hippocratic corpus mentions a boy who "became a eunuch from hunting and running" (*Epidemics* 7.122). Aristotle—especially as the son of a physician—would likely have known of accidental castration, and its effects on the unfortunate person castrated. Similarly, Aristotle notes that some men (and women) born with "mutilated" (i.e., deformed, πηρωθῶσι) genitalia are sterile from birth, and as a result the men "never grow a beard, but remain eunuch-like" (εὐνουχίας) (*GA* 2.7.746b20–24).[7] The similarity between eunuchs and women was a topic of scientific interest, and Aristotle would likely have known of other references to eunuchs in the Hippocratic writings.[8] *On Seed* gives an explanation for the impotence of eunuchs (2.1–6), while *Nature of the Child* discusses why eunuchs and women are hairless on their chins and bodies and why eunuchs do not become bald (20).[9]

Finally, Aristotle's closest exposure to castration and its effects must have been his own research on the castration of animals. For example, *History of Animals* 8 (9).50 is a long chapter devoted, for the most part, to the effects of castration. In it, Aristotle discusses the castration of birds, oviparous quadrupeds, boars, deer, bulls, and humans, often in some detail.[10]

Living when and where Aristotle lived and given people's closer contact with livestock farmers, the castration of animals in general, and even the mutilation of boys to produce eunuchs, were relatively well-known phenomena. It seems that, as a result, there arose at that time the practice of eunuch metaphor.

Athenaeus tells us that the Pythagoreans referred to one kind of lettuce as "eunuch" lettuce (69e)—probably because it was thought to check sexual desire.[11] He also tells us that Plato Comicus, in his *Laios,* calls melons without seeds "eunuch-like" (68c = fr. 64 Kock). He reports that Aristotle, in the (lost) work *On Plants,* writes that "some call [seedless dates] 'eunuchs' and others 'stoneless'" (652a = fr. 267 Rose). Finally, Aristotle's suc-

---

7. In this same chapter, Aristotle refers to both masculine-looking women (γυναῖκες ἀρρενωποὶ) and effeminate men (ἄνδρες θηλυκοί) as mutilations or deformities (πηρώματα) (746b31–747a3).

8. I cannot here discuss the nature of the Hippocratic corpus or the dates of the individual works within it. I follow Lloyd: "Most of the material in the gynaecological treatises can be dated no more precisely than to the late fifth or the fourth century B.C." (1983, 63n10).

9. The Hippocratic *Aphorisms* states: "Eunuchs are not subject to gout, nor do they go bald" (6.28).

10. See also *HA* 3.1.510a35–b4; *GA* 1.2.716b5–13, 5.7.787b19–788a16; and *Problems* 10.36, 57.

11. See Pliny *Natural History* 19.127.

cessor in the Lyceum, Theophrastus, discussing reeds, says that those without a plume or flower tufts (ἀνθήλη) are called "eunuchs" (*Historia plantarum* 4.11.4).

Evidently, the use of eunuch metaphors to describe natural phenomena (or at the very least, plants) was not uncommon. If, in this context, eunuch metaphors or analogies proved to have explanatory power, then it would be unreasonable to conclude that any comparison between females and mutilated males in the natural sciences must have been ideologically motivated. So, did Aristotle's analogy between females and castrated males—women and eunuchs—have explanatory power?

USING EUNUCHS TO EXPLAIN WOMEN

Let me begin by quoting part of *HA* 8 (9).50, Aristotle's most sustained discussion of castration.

> The animals change their forms and character not only, in certain cases, according to their ages and the seasons, but also through being castrated. Castration can be done to any animals that have testicles. . . . The birds are castrated at the rump, at the point where they come together in mating; for after cauterizing them there with two or three irons, if the bird is already full-grown, the crest becomes pale yellow and he no longer crows nor tries to mate, while if he is still a young bird none of these characteristics even develops as he grows. It is the same way with men. For if they have been mutilated as boys the later-growing hair does not develop nor does the voice change but continues high-pitched; but if they are already past puberty the later-growing hair falls out except for the pubic hair (and this diminishes but remains), but the congenital hair does not fall out; for no eunuch becomes bald.[12] The voice changes too into the female even in all quadrupeds that are castrated or mutilated. (631b19–632a7)

This passage shows that Aristotle was familiar, either directly or indirectly, with a range of castrated animals (including eunuchs); he was familiar with the procedures used to castrate at least some of these animals; and he was aware that the changes that result from castration do not simply involve the mutilated area (i.e., the testicles), but that castration also changes many other physical attributes.

---

12. Dorfman and Shipley point out that there can be significant differences between the results of prepuberal and postpuberal castration (1956, 305, 321–22).

Aristotle concluded from his observations about castration that just as a relatively small change to the body of an animal can affect the whole animal, so a small change in the development of an embryo could affect not only the area that was directly changed but also the physical nature of the whole animal that results. We see this conclusion stated at least four times in the biological writings. In *HA* 7 (8).2, Aristotle writes: "Through undergoing a change in small parts, animals appear to have a major difference in the nature of their whole bodies. This is clear in the case of castrated animals: for after a small part has been mutilated, the animal changes over towards the female; so that it is clear that in the animal's original constitution [ἐν τῇ ἐξ ἀρχῆς συστάσει] too, if some tiny part changes in a major way, provided that it is an originative part [ἀρχοειδές], one becomes female and another male, and if it is wholly destroyed, the animal becomes neither" (589b31–590a5). In *GA* 1.2, toward the beginning of his discussion of male and female, Aristotle writes:

> If a small principle [μικρᾶς ἀρχῆς] is altered, many of the things depending on the principle usually change with it. This is clear in the case of castrated animals: for although the generative part alone is destroyed, almost the whole shape [of the animal] changes with it to such an extent that it seems to be female or to fall just short of that, so that it is not in respect of some random part and some random capacity that the animal is female or male. Thus it is evident that the female and the male are shown to be principles. (716b3–10)

He makes this same point in *GA* 4.1, in a discussion of the determination of sex during the development of the embryo (766a25–30), and in *GA* 5.7, where he describes the differences between males and females with respect to voice (788a7–16).

Aristotle moves from the fact that castration—a change in a relatively small part of the body—affects the whole body, to the idea that a small change in an embryo (or in the development of an embryo) can account for differences between males and females. Let us pursue in greater detail the connection Aristotle sees concerning the contrast between normal and castrated males, on the one hand, and normal males and females, on the other.

Generation of Animals 5.7 is devoted to voice, and a fair amount of it deals with the differences between male and female voices. Here is one section:

All animals, when castrated, change over to the female, and as their sinewy strength is slackened at its principle they emit a voice similar to that of females. This slackening may be illustrated in the following way. It is as though you were to stretch a cord and make it taut by hanging some weight on to it, just as women do who weave at the loom; they stretch the warp by hanging stone weights on to it. This is the way in which the testes are attached to the spermatic passages. . . . If the testes are removed, the tautness of the passages is slackened, just as when the weight is removed from the cord or from the warp; and as this slackens, the principle which sets the voice in movement is correspondingly loosened. This then is the cause on account of which castrated animals change over to the female both as regards voice and the rest of their form: it is because the principle from which the tautness of the body is derived is slackened. . . . Small alterations are the causes of big ones, not in virtue of themselves, but when it happens that a principle changes at the same time. For the principles, though small in size, are great in capacity: that is what it is to be a principle—something which is itself a cause of many things, while there is nothing more ultimate which is the cause of it. (787b19–788a16)[13]

This discussion is of course inaccurate in its details. But it is accurate in that there are differences between male and female voices, and similarly between the voices of normal and castrated males. Ralph I. Dorfman and Reginald A. Shipley, in their book *Androgens: Biochemistry, Physiology, and Clinical Significance,* write: "The voice [of a castrated or eunichoid male] retains its juvenile high pitch because of the failure of the larynx to enlarge, and of the vocal cords to lengthen" (1956, 319). Further, it is clear that Aristotle is trying to explain genuine differences in the voices of males and females by reference to what can be observed about castrated animals.

Aristotle also uses facts about eunuchs to explain the differences between men and women with respect to the (in)capacity to go bald: "Women do not go bald, for their nature is similar to that of children: both are incapable of producing spermatic secretions. Eunuchs, too, do not go bald, because of their transition into the female, and the hair that comes at a later stage they fail to grow at all, or if they already have it, they lose it, except for the pubic hair: similarly, women do not have the later hair, though they do grow the pubic hair. This mutilation [πήϱωσις] constitutes a change from the male to the female" (*GA* 5.3.784a4–11; cf. 782a9–11). Aris-

13. See also *GA* 1.4.717a34–b4.

totle concluded that it must be a similarity between eunuchs and females that accounts for the fact that both eunuchs and females do not go bald, whereas men can.[14]

Observations of the effects of castration on certain animals, together with observations of the difference between males and females regarding defensive parts (e.g., horns), strengthen the analogy between females and mutilated males. In *HA* 8 (9).50, Aristotle writes: "If deer are castrated when they do not yet have horns because of their age, then they never grow horns; but if they already have them when castrated, the size of the horns remains the same and they do not cast them" (632a10–13).[15] In *HA* 4.11, he says: "With respect to those parts that exist by nature with a view to defense, e.g., teeth, tusks, horns, spurs and parts such as these, in some kinds of animals the males alone have them and the females do not. . . . In other kinds they belong to both, but they are much better in males, e.g., the horns of bulls are stronger than those of cows" (538b15–24; see also *PA* 3.1.661b26–662a5). It is likely that in a full account of why it is that, among deer (or at least the ones Aristotle was acquainted with), the buck grows horns while the doe does not, Aristotle would have made reference to the effect of castration on a young buck. How is it that the doe comes to have no horns? Part of the answer is teleological, of course: the buck needs them for combat, the doe does not, and nature does nothing in vain. But part of the account might include the following: just as a change in a small part of the buck led to a big change—that is, castration led to its not growing any horns—so a small change in the course of the development of a fetus

14. Dorfman and Shipley write:
Growth of the adult beard is entirely lacking in the hypogonadal subject. Other areas which fail to develop course pigmented hair of normal length are the extremities, chest, lower abdomen, scrotum, and peranal region. The shafts remain thin, straight, poorly pigmented, and retain the appearance of fine sparse down as seen in the juvenile state. Pubic and axillary hair, on the other hand, are not completely absent in simple testicular failure. Adrenal androgens are sufficiently potent to stimulate considerable development in these two regions. The growth over the pubis resembles that of a female. The pattern is small and the upper border horizontal. Axillary hair tends to be sparse but is not completely absent. . . . The hair of the scalp is somewhat fine in texture, and the frontal border appears as an uninterrupted curve without the usual wedge-shaped indentations which are present over the sides of the forehead in the normal adult. Extensive simple baldness does not occur. (1956, 318–19)

15. The Aristotelian *Problems* remarks on the effects of castration on rams (their horns become smaller than normal) and bulls (their horns become bigger than normal) (10.36, 57). The reasons given for the difference in change are interesting but cannot be discussed here.

caused it to be female instead of male and, thus (among other effects), to lack horns.

In *HA* 4.11, Aristotle describes further differences between males and females: "The female is more lacking in muscle and weaker in joints [or less articulated, ἀναρθρότερον], and thinner in hair (in those kinds of animals that have hair). . . . Also, females have flabbier [or suppler or softer] flesh [ὑγροσαρκότερα] than males and walk more with their knees together, and their shins are thinner. And their feet are smoother (among animals that have such parts)" (538b7–12). This passage bears comparing to Aristotle's discussion of voice in *GA* 5.7, where he writes: "In all animals, their strength is in their sinews, and that is why animals in their prime are stronger than the others: young ones are less well articulated and less well supplied with sinews, and furthermore, their sinews have not yet become taut" (787b10–12). As we have seen, Aristotle sees a causal connection between castration and the loss of the tautness of sinew: "All animals, when castrated, change over to the female, and as their sinewy strength is slackened at its principle they emit a voice similar to that of females" (*GA* 5.7.787b19–22). This is most likely related to Aristotle's claim that "all animals if castrated young become . . . smoother [γλαφυρώτερα] than the uncastrated" (*HA* 8 [9].50.632a8–9).[16]

Aristotle notes that normal males tend to be physically stronger, more muscular, and not as soft as castrated males; and he is correct. Dorfman and Shipley describe "the accumulation of fat in particular areas in the eunuch," which include "the ventral abdominal wall on the area surmounting the symphysis pubis, around the mammary glands, on the lateral surfaces of the upper portion of the thigh, and about the buttocks," and "over the upper aspects of the arms and the shoulders" (1956, 210). Further, they write that "muscular development and strength are relatively poor compared to the normal adult male" (315). In postpuberal castrates, where the change in physical form is not so radical, it is still the case that "physical endurance may be impaired" (322). So Aristotle again sees, correctly, a parallel between the differences between normal and castrated males, on the one hand, and males and females, on the other.

Concerning the height of castrated males, Dorfman and Shipley write: "In most instances, but not invariably, the stature is above average because of a disproportionate increase in length of the long bones" (1956, 315). Ar-

16. See *GA* 1.19.727a10–15.

istotle recognizes this difference in height in a passage from *HA* 8 (9).50: "All animals if castrated young become bigger and smoother than the uncastrated, but if their development is already complete they do not grow any more additionally" (632a8–10). So Aristotle is aware of an apparent exception to the women-eunuch analogy, for women in fact tend to be shorter than men. Can he account for it?

The author of *Problems* 10.36 writes:

Why is it that eunuchs, when they are disabled [i.e., castrated] (διαφθει-ρόμενοι), in other respects change into the female? For they have feminine voice, shapelessness [or shrillness], and lack of articulation (καὶ γὰρ φωνὴν θηλυκὴν ἴσχουσιν καὶ ἀμορφίαν [or ὀξύτητα] καὶ ἀναρθίαν),[17] and so undergo a severe change, as do other animals when castrated. . . . But in respect to size alone, eunuchs change into the male, for they become larger. And this is characteristic of the male, for females are smaller than males. Or is this not a change into the male, but into the female? For it is not a change in every [aspect of] size, but in height alone, whereas [change into] the male is [a change] in width and depth as well; for this is what it is to be full grown. Furthermore, as the female is to the male, so within the female gender itself the maiden is to the woman; for the latter is already nobly formed, while the former is not. So [the maiden] changes into [the nature of women], for their growth is with respect to height.[18] This is why Homer speaks well: "chaste Artemis gave them height," being able to give what she possessed in virtue of her maidenhood. Therefore, the eunuch does not change, with respect to size, into the male. For he does not change into what is complete. Eunuchs increase in size only with respect to height (894b19–38).

17. This passage has been read in two ways: (1) eunuchs have feminine voices, shapeless (i.e., less well defined or muscular?) bodies, and loose joints; or (2) the passage refers solely to speech and states that eunuchs have feminine, shrill (reading ὀξύτητα rather than ἀμορφίαν), and less articulate voices; see Flashar (1962, 520). Which reading is better is of little consequence for my purposes here.

18. The Greek is: εἰς τὴν τούτων οὖν μεταβάλλει ἐπὶ μῆκος γὰρ ταύταις ἡ αὔξησις. I take there to be an implied φύσιν, i.e., εἰς τὴν τούτων φύσιν ("into their nature"); see Flashar (1962, 520). If this is correct, then there are two ways to take this passage: (1) the eunuch changes into the nature of women or (2) the maiden changes into the nature of women. (That is, "their growth" would refer to either the eunuchs' growth or that of the maidens.) I believe the second option is most likely correct, especially given the quote from Homer (*Odyssey* 20.71); but whichever is right does not ultimately affect my interpretation of the chapter.

The author of this passage seems to be making the following point: castration causes the male to grow taller. But this does not mean the eunuch is developing more like the male than like the female with respect to height. When a boy becomes a man, he grows in height, width, and depth. When a girl becomes a woman, she grows in height (but not, relative to the man, in width and depth—or, not to the degree that a man does). When a eunuch grows taller, he resembles a maiden growing into a woman, not a boy growing into a man. Thus, the Aristotelian can argue, the value and applicability of the eunuch-analogy is preserved.

Whatever remains unclear here, the author's point is that since the eunuch does not change into a male with respect to size in general (i.e., with respect to height, width, depth, and shape) but with respect to height alone, this does not constitute an exception (or at least not a major exception) to the analogy between women and eunuchs. If the author of this chapter is Aristotle, then the important points are (1) he did not ignore the fact that eunuchs tend to grow taller than normal males, a fact that might be taken as an exception to his eunuch-female analogy, and (2) he did not, in my view, engage in blatantly bad reasoning or rationalization. The *Problems* 10.36 passage is a decent attempt to show how a eunuch's height is not really the same as a normal man's height.

CASTRATING IDEOLOGY

As we saw in the previous chapter, Aristotle believed that in generation, the movements from the father work on the matter from the mother. If the movements from the mother overpower those from the father—at least those pertaining to the determination of sex—the result is a female: that is, a less muscular, less "articulated," softer version of the animal. I believe he would claim that this position is justified, in part, from the fact that eunuchs, as a result of castration, are less muscular, taut, "articulated," softer, and more effeminate than normal males.

Briefly discussing the infamous line with which we began this chapter, Jonathan Barnes describes what might well be the standard reaction to it: "How vile, cry the critics. Even Aristotle's friends are embarrassed. . . . The pejorative term 'mutilated' has no place in a scientific treatise and its appearance in Aristotle's text is a regrettable rhetorical manifestation of latent prejudice." He continues, in his own voice: "The friends concede too much. Aristotle's view has a decent empirical basis. . . . Mutilated males acquire female characteristics (high voice, soft skin, and so on): hence females are, so to speak, mutilated males. The argument may be less than probative, but it is gratuitous to discount it as a cloak and a pretext for prejudice" (1984a, 9). Barnes is right. Whatever Aristotle's conception of females at the outset of his scientific investigations, there is no evidence that he began with some (explicit or implicit) ideologically slanted view of women as mutilated, and read that into his biology. It is much more likely that he observed what he did about eunuchs and castrated animals and concluded that eunuchs are similar to women—females are like mutilated males—in a number of interesting ways. Further, he saw that such an analogy went a long way toward explaining how a small difference at the beginning of the development of an embryo could lead to the relatively big differences that we observe between the parts of male and the parts of female adults.

APPENDIX: COGNITION AND SOFTER FLESH

Aristotle makes the uncontroversial claim that women and eunuchs tend to have softer flesh than normal males. This could pose a problem for him, when considered in light of a passage from DA 2.9:

> This sense [i.e., touch] is the most accurate in the human [τὸν ἄνθρω-πον]; for in the other [senses, the human] is inferior to many animals, but in respect of touch [the human] far excels the others in accuracy. This is why [the human] is the most intelligent [φρονιμώτατον] of animals. A sign of this is the fact that within the human race, natural endowment and the lack of it depend on this sense organ [i.e., the organ of touch] and on no other; for those with hard flesh are poorly endowed with thought [διάνοιαν], while those with soft flesh [μαλακόσαρκοι] are well endowed. (421a19–26) [19]

Cynthia Freeland notes: "Aristotle has claimed that soft flesh accounts for intelligence, and accurate discrimination among men. Why not in women?" (1992, 235). Actually, Aristotle refers to humans, not just men, in this De anima passage; but that does not solve his problem. He here says that among humans, those with softer flesh tend to be more intelligent than those with harder flesh, which would mean—if he were consistent—that women and eunuchs would tend to be better endowed with intelligence than normal men.

---

19. On humans possessing the softest flesh, see also PA 2.16.660a11–14.

There are a number of ways of taking *DA* 2.9, 421a19–26. First, this passage is evidence that when Aristotle says "human," he means "man" not "woman" (the imperfect human). If this were the case, it could be evidence of ideological bias; for not only does it sound ideologically tainted in itself, it does not address the problem: imperfect or not, if women have softer flesh, given what Aristotle says, they should tend to be more intelligent than men.

Second, the passage contradicts what Aristotle says elsewhere about women. Aristotle's claim that women and eunuchs tend to have softer flesh than normal men contradicts his claim that among humans, softer flesh means greater intelligence. Point 2b of the test for ideological rationalization states that contradiction is evidence of bias. Is that the conclusion to come to here? It's hard to say. On the one hand, Aristotle does not maintain a contradiction in order to defend a view that is antiwoman; in fact, the contradiction involves a position that seems to suggest that women are more intelligent than men. On the other hand, we can with justice ask why Aristotle did not revise his position on either female intelligence or the connection between soft flesh and intelligence. Freeland, perhaps hoping to save Aristotle here, claims that what he said about soft flesh and intelligence in *DA* 2.9 may have been provisional. Now that may be the case, though I see little evidence for it.[20] It remains possible that Aristotle held the contradiction described here owing to gender bias.

Finally, there is a plausible reading of this passage that avoids any contradiction: it is possible that Aristotle does think women have a more accurate and discriminating sense of touch, but since she otherwise lacks the intellectual potentialities of normal men, this superior discrimination

---

20. Discussing *DA* 421a19–26, Freeland writes: "This should be taken with a grain of salt because Aristotle offers several alternative explanations for humans' superior intelligence, most notably standing upright (*PA* 4.10), having a large brain (for cooling, to balance our sensitive sense-organs in the head; *PA* 2.7); having acute hearing, which is incidentally relevant because of its role in understanding voiced signs, or language (*HA* 608a17–21); and having the finest, most supple tongue (which also plays a role in language; *PA* 660a15–28)" (1992, 234). These passages, however, do not show either that Aristotle contradicts himself or that his claim about soft flesh and intelligence is provisional. For Aristotle could maintain that the characteristics Freeland mentions—plus soft flesh—are *all* causes of human intelligence. But more important, standing upright and so forth are not Aristotle's explanations for human intelligence; rather, human intelligence is Aristotle's explanation for standing upright et cetera. On intelligence and standing upright in humans, see Lennox (2001a, 317–18).

cannot produce the greater intelligence that is found in men. Further, this more accurate sense of touch might in part explain why Aristotle believes the female has a greater sensitivity to pain. (See the discussions of softness and of female cognition in chap. 6.) In conclusion, I would say that we here have a possible case of ideological bias but no obvious contradiction.

FIVE

In his biological works, Aristotle makes a number of seemingly bizarre statements about the differences between the parts of males and the parts of females—most notoriously, he says that females have fewer teeth than males.[1] These remarks have not escaped the notice of scholars, many of whom assume that Aristotle arrived at these conclusions by applying biased generalizations rather than engaging in proper, empirical research. For example, Martha Nussbaum writes: "I believe Aristotle's biology is . . . both misogynist and silly." She adds, however, that "the fact that Aristotle *said stupid things without looking,* despite his evident genius for looking . . . , is not a deep defect in either his methodology or the substance of his scientific thought" (1998, 249–50, emphasis added). G. E. R. Lloyd claims that Aristotle's biases led him "to a number of superficial and some quite inaccurate statements on anatomical points which it should not have been too hard to check" (1983, 102). Lesley Ann Dean-Jones believes the principle "that the female is a less perfect representative of the human form than the male" led Aristotle to make certain "erroneous claims" (1994, 81). Nussbaum, Lloyd, and Dean-Jones all give Aristotle's infamous remarks about teeth as an example.

So some scholars conclude that whatever else we might say about Aristotle's biology, he sometimes came to stupid conclusions—conclusions he could have avoided had he looked—because of the sexist assumptions

---

1. I shall not attempt to explain these bizarre statements by appealing to the possibility that they are later interpolations by someone other than Aristotle. That would, I expect, appear tendentious. Nevertheless, in some cases this might be a distinct possibility. See William Ogle's arguments along these lines (quoted extensively in app. A at the end of this chapter).

he followed.[2] Granted that these views seem bizarre to us and (in most cases) are false, I want to show that, for the most part, there is no reason to assume that they were the result of ideological rationalization, whereby Aristotle came to the conclusions he did in the absence (or in defiance) of observation. I shall look at five claims: that females have (1) smaller brains, (2) different skulls, (3) paler skin, (4) softer bones, and (5) fewer teeth than males.[3]

Keep in mind that whatever differences Aristotle claimed existed between male parts and female parts, he also maintained that the whole animal is not male or female—only certain parts—and that male and female do not differ in species.[4]

SMALLER BRAINS

In *PA* 2.7, Aristotle writes that "among human beings the males have a larger brain than the females" (653a28–29). This sounds serious.

Deborah Blum, in *Sex on the Brain,* writes: "More than any other gender comparison in biology, it's fair to say that feminist scholars hate this one [i.e., the comparison of brain size] the most. Brown University geneticist Anne Fausto-Sterling argues that the work is biased from its start; male scientists consistently find that male scientists have the biggest brains" (1997, 38). Fausto-Sterling's claim is not only strange, it also poisons the well. For how is a male scientist to react if the male brain is in fact larger than the female? (How would a male geneticist react to the "charge" that male geneticists consistently find that the male contribution to generation is variable and, thus, determines the offspring's gender?) Blum dismisses the Fausto-Sterling approach and applauds efforts to answer questions about relative brain size, such as what that size is and why. Nevertheless, she points out that, historically, biased scientists *have* often concluded that male brain size is larger and then automatically linked this finding to what they see as the differing intellectual capacities of males and females.[5]

---

2. Dean-Jones (1994, 81–82) approaches, but falls short of, this attitude toward Aristotle.

3. Actually, the first three claims apply to women, not females generally. The last two apply to females of a limited number of kinds of animals, including humans. Note also that not all of the claims dealt with in this chapter are the subject of controversy; but they all could be, so I thought it was worthwhile devoting space to them.

4. On the first claim, see *GA* 1.2.716a27–31; on the second, see *Metaphysics* 10.9 and *GA* 1.23.730b33–731a1.

5. Blum 1998, chap. 2; see also Richardson 1997.

Blum does not mention Aristotle as part of this history, but some scholars have. Nancy Tuana describes Aristotle's seemingly tendentious claim as follows: "Woman's defect of heat results in her brain being smaller and less developed, and her inferior brain size in turn accounts for much of her defective nature. Woman's less concocted brain renders her deliberative faculty too ineffective to rule over her emotions" (1994, 202–3). Froma Zeitlin, too, sees a connection between Aristotle's conception of male and female brains and their differences (in his view) in intellect (1988, 66).

But the attribution of this line of thinking to Aristotle is simply wrong. There is no evidence that his claim that the man's brain is larger than the woman's has the cognitive significance Tuana and Zeitlin suggest it does.

Aristotle's most extended discussion of the brain is in *PA* 2.7. He there writes that the brain "is present in animals for the preservation of their entire nature" (652b6–7)—which it does in the following way: "Everything requires an opposing counterweight in order that it achieve the moderate state and the mean (for the mean possesses substantial being and the definite account, while each of the extremes separately does not)—because of this, nature has devised the brain in relation to the heart's location and heat. . . . The brain, then, makes the heat and boiling in the heart well-tempered" (652b17–28). So the purpose of the brain is to regulate the temperature of the heart. The human cognitive functions that we now know are connected to the brain, Aristotle located in the heart.[6] But why is it that "among human beings the males have a larger brain than the females"? Aristotle tells us: "For the region around the heart and the lung is also most hot and most sanguineous in males" (*PA* 2.7.653a29–30). The reason for this, presumably, is that males tend to be bigger than females—and thus tend to have more blood in that region—and (he believes) that males tend to have warmer blood (as we saw in chap. 3).

Now one could try to argue for a connection between larger brains and diminished cognitive capacities, in Aristotle's view, by focusing on the connection between the brain and the heart. Although he believes that "the brain has no connection to any one of the perceptual parts" (*PA* 2.7.652b3), there is nevertheless a connection between the brain and the heart—and thus sensation. In *PA* 3.11, he says that the heart and the brain "most of all control life" (673b11–12). In a number of places, he makes it clear that there

---

6. See *PA* 2.10. On the cognitive functions being located not in the brain but in the heart, see 656a15–35.

is some connection between the brain and the senses and even among the brain, the heart, certain senses, and the blood being well proportioned (this last being the brain's function).[7] So it is just possible that Aristotle saw a connection between the larger size of the brain and a superior functioning of the senses. If so, this would be a case of ideological bias affecting his biology. There is, however, no direct evidence for attributing such a belief to him. Aristotle never actually makes a connection between cognition and larger brain size, as Tuana seems to think he does. So Aristotle's claim that the man's brain is larger than the woman's—a claim that is most likely true—does not have any obvious ideological implications for his biology.[8]

DIFFERENT SKULLS

Lloyd writes that Aristotle "makes some fairly elementary blunders" and gives, as an example, Aristotle's statement "concerning . . . the sutures of the skull in women" (1983, 104).[9] What did Aristotle say on this subject, and what may have led him to say it?

In *HA* 1.7, Aristotle writes: "The skull has sutures: one, of circular form, in the case of women; in the case of men, as a general rule, three meeting at a point. Instances have been known of a man's skull devoid of suture altogether. In the skull, the middle line, where the hair parts, is called the crown or vertex" (491b2–6). Similarly, *HA* 3.7 says: "[The skull] is not the same in all animals. In some, the skull consists of a single bone, as in the dog, while in others it is composite, as in the human. Among [humans], the female has a circular suture, whereas the male has three sutures that join together at the top, like a triangle, and instances have been known of a man's skull being devoid of suture altogether" (516a15–20). This exception may come from Herodotus. Recording what the Plataeans reported they had seen when the flesh had fallen away or been removed from the bodies of the Persian dead (who had been killed in battle), he says:

---

7. Aristotle makes a connection between the brain and the senses in *PA* 2.7.653b5–8, 2.10.656b22–26, *HA* 1.2.492a19–22, 1.16.495a11–18, 2.12.503b17, *De sensu* 2.438b25–30. He connects the brain, the heart, and certain senses with the blood being well proportioned in *PA* 2.10.656a37–b19, 4.10.686a5–13.

8. Ogle (1882, 167n18) thought that the issue of whether the man's brain is larger than the woman's was unresolved. (He seems to be followed by Lloyd [1983, 102n167].) But recent studies have yielded more conclusive results. Ann Gibbons reports: "Men's brains are on average larger than women's by 15%—about twice the difference in average body size between men and women" (1991, 958). See also Ankey 1992; Richardson 1997; Blum 1998, chap. 2.

9. See also Dean-Jones 1994, 81.

"There was found a skull without suture, but all of one bone" (9.83, in Grene 1987). Battlefield observations were very likely a typical way of getting information about the internal makeup of human beings.

Continuing the *PA* 2.7 passage on brains quoted in the previous section, Aristotle explains why he thinks the man has more sutures than the woman: "[The human] also has many sutures around the head, and the male more than the females, for the same reason, in order that this place is well-ventilated, and more so the larger the brain" (653a29–b3).

But Aristotle is wrong: The skulls of men and women have the same number of sutures. The question is: Why was Aristotle mistaken? Did he engage in armchair biology, in which case we might suspect his motives in coming up with this difference? Or might there have been a more honest reason for his error?

William Ogle provides an explanation for how Aristotle might have come to this erroneous conclusion while at the same time being committed to the importance of observation.

> Of course the opportunities of seeing a female skull would be much fewer than of seeing a male skull; for battle fields would no longer be of service. Still it is not impossible that A.'s statement may have been founded on some single observation. For it is by no means uncommon for the sutures on the vertex to become more or less effaced in pregnant women; so common indeed is it, that the name "puerperal osteophyte" has been given to the condition by Rokitansky.... A woman's skull may have been observed in which the Sagittal suture had thus disappeared; when the Lamboid, with the lateral sutures, and the Coronal, might fairly be described as forming together a circular suture. It must not be forgotten what great difficulty there was in A.'s time in getting a sight of human bones. (1882, 168n26)[10]

So let us speculate (since that's all we can do here) about what kind of case Aristotle might have had for his claim about human sutures. Keep in mind this last point of Ogle's: there were probably not many opportunities—especially outside of the battlefield—for observing human skulls. This would have been especially true of women's skulls, which one would have been less likely to encounter on the battlefield. So Aristotle must have

---

10. Ogle's point is cited in Lloyd (1983, 102n165) and Dean-Jones (1994, 81); see Lennox (2001a, 211–12). D. W. Thompson writes: "I imagine that this singular misstatement dates from a belief that the sutures of the skull coincided with the margin and the partings of the hairy scalp" (1910, ad 491b4, n. 7).

seen (or at least heard about) a fairly limited number of skulls, and he probably saw men's skulls much more often than women's. In the case of men's skulls, Aristotle accurately observed the three sutures (and noted an exception—a case in which the man had fewer sutures than what he concluded was the case for a typical woman). Following Ogle's lead, we can speculate that Aristotle perhaps had the opportunity to examine only a single female skull—or at any rate, not likely more than a couple—which came from a woman (or women) who died in childbirth or during a complicated pregnancy. He observed one suture in this skull (or these skulls) and so concluded that a man normally had three sutures, whereas a woman had only one.

It counts against Aristotle that he ignored or rejected the Hippocratic text *On the Wounds in the Head* (assuming he read it), which does not distinguish between the number of sutures in men and in women, and whose author apparently had observed a number of skulls. But had Aristotle made the observations described in the above speculation, he would no doubt have replied that he had evidence that the author of *On the Wounds in the Head* was mistaken—though it would have been dubious of Aristotle to reject those findings on the basis of the observation of one or two female human skulls.

This speculation that Aristotle observed one (or two) female human skull(s), and that it (or they each) possessed only one suture, is more plausible than the claim that Aristotle ignored evidence or simply did not bother to gather any—that he instead concluded arbitrarily that women have one circular suture rather than the three that form a triangle in the skulls of men. My guess is that Aristotle observed a female human skull with one suture and that he could easily explain this difference given his view of the brain, as he does in *PA* 2.7 (though had he observed that men and women always had the same number of sutures, that would not have proved problematic): the larger the brain, the more ventilation required; the more ventilation required, the greater the number of sutures in the skull; thus, it makes sense that nature gave man more sutures than woman.

But what would be the ideological motive for coming up with such an argument with little or no evidence supporting it? Of course, one can always construct an ideological scenario wherein Aristotle was led to conclude what he did. For example, the greater the cognitive abilities (he would supposedly have argued), the larger the brain; the larger the brain, the more ventilation required; the more ventilation required, the greater the number of sutures in the skull; thus, man has more sutures than woman

because of his greater cognitive abilities. But as in the case of male and female brains, there is no evidence that Aristotle thought along such lines.
It is much more likely that he was led to conclude what he did from his
observations of available skulls—however insufficient these observations
may have been, whatever Hippocratic accounts he may have dismissed, and
however premature he may have been in coming to a conclusion based on
so few samples.

PALER SKIN

In *GA* 1.19, Aristotle writes that the "woman discharges more [menses]
than other animals. That is why she is conspicuously pale [ἐπιδηλοτάτως
. . . ὠχρόν]" (727a22–24). It is clear from the context of this passage that
Aristotle regards women as paler than men (and than females of other animal kinds) and that he believes this is part of their nature. Besides the reason he gives—the quantity of menses discharged—what else may have led
him to this conclusion?

I initially assumed that Aristotle was simply following Greek convention, and this may turn out to be true. I'll explore such an interpretation of
the passage, before turning to another possible way of explaining it.

Ancient Greek women—or at least the women of better-off Greek
citizens—stayed indoors and, thus, remained relatively fair skinned; the
men, in contrast, spent most of their time outdoors and, thus, were
darker than the women. At the beginning of Aristophanes' *Ecclesiazusae,*
the women of Athens are preparing to sneak into the assembly, dressed as
men. Their leader asks if they have made the necessary preparations. One
woman answers: "I oiled my whole body and tanned myself, standing in
the sun the whole day" (62–64; see also 124–27). This part of the plan was
not entirely successful because we later find that the women are still described as whiter than normal men (385–87, 427–30).[11] In Xenophon's
Oeconomica, book 10, the husband says his wife uses white lead to make
herself appear whiter (λευκοτέρα) and rouge for a more rosy complexion
(πολλῇ ἐγχούσῃ), and this was a common practice.[12] The husband complains that this is deceitful, and he tells her how to achieve a genuine
healthy complexion (εὔχρως):

11. Translation from Mayhew 1997a. See Ussher 1973, 83, 93, 129–30. At Aristophanes
Thesmophoriazusae 191 and *Ecclesiazusae* 427–30, paleness in men is a sign of effeminacy.

12. See also Aristophanes *Lysistrata* 42–48, and Pomeroy (1994, 304–5).

I advised her not to spend her time sitting around like a slave, but, with the help of the gods, to try to stand before the loom as a mistress of a household should, and furthermore to teach anything that she knew better than anyone else, and to learn anything that she knew less well; to supervise the baker, and to stand next to the housekeeper while she was measuring out provisions, and also to go around inspecting whether everything was where it ought to be. These activities, I thought, combined her domestic concerns with a walk. (2–3, 5, 10–11, Pomeroy 1994)

Note that his advice requires that she spend most of her time indoors.

Sarah Pomeroy provides a good summary of the expectation among Greeks that women should be paler than men (and the use of cosmetics to achieve this): "Despite its toxicity lead carbonate was used to whiten the complexion. Respectable women ideally spent their time indoors, though some in unfortunate circumstances had to perform work out of doors. . . . Therefore a fair skin marked a woman as a member of the leisured class. This idea of beauty can be traced as far back in the eastern Mediterranean world as the frescoes of Cnossus and Thera, where women are portrayed with white skin and men with suntanned flesh" (1994, 305).

If Aristotle is simply following Greek convention in the above *GA* 1.19 passage, then his belief that women are paler than men is probably biased. For if he is (falsely) attributing a deficiency to women, without any strong evidence, we should certainly be suspicious of some level of gender prejudice.[13] And Aristotle's claim would seem to be supported by an arbitrary assumption, namely, that the way things are for most (or the better-off) Greeks is the way things are naturally: men are darker in skin color than women. Further, his belief also seems to be supported by an unusually bad argument (for Aristotle) because he deduces the conclusion from what he takes to be a fact about menses (that it is abundant in women compared to females of other animal kinds) while ignoring facts that were readily available. First, it does not take an Aristotle to know that the sun at least in part determines whether a person is tanned or pale. Second, Aristotle knew (or should have known) that not all Greek women were pale, since poor women (not to mention female slaves) would have spent a great deal of time outdoors. (Note that in *Pol.* 6.8 he writes: "The poor must employ

13. The author(s) of *Problems* connects being pale (ὠχρόν) with a departure of heat (27.8), and calls pallor or lack of color (ἄχροια) a corruption (38.4). Darkness, however, is possibly considered a sign of decay (38.9). But for Aristotle (and for most Greeks) the paleness of women is certainly considered a deficiency compared to the skin color of men.

their women and children as servants, because of their lack of slaves" [1323a5–6].) Third, Aristotle knew of non-Greek cultures—for example, the Ethiopians—in which the women could not reasonably be described as pale at all.

But I would like to suggest an alternative interpretation, which I think is even more plausible (though I can claim little with certainty here). I begin with an analysis of two Greek words, both of which are sometimes translated as "pale": λευκόν and ὠχρός. (Throughout, I translate them "white" and "pale," respectively.) According to LSJ, λευκόν means "white," and it is the opposite of μέλαν (usually translated "black" or "dark"); ὠχρός means "pale" or "wan," when speaking of complexion, and "pale yellow" or "yellow" generally. (Ὁ ὦχρος refers to paleness, and especially "the pale hue of fear.")

Aristotle's use of these two terms seems pretty close to what we find in LSJ. First, he holds that λευκόν and μέλαν are opposites, whereas ὠχρός has no opposite (*Categories* 8.10b13–17, 10.12a17–19, *Metaphysics* 10.5.1056a26–30). Generally, he does not use λευκόν and ὠχρός as synonyms. For example, he says that the testicles in some kinds of animals are white, whereas others are pale (*HA* 3.1.509b26); some eggs are white, some pale, and some are other colors (*HA* 6.2.559a23–24). Of course, he (or the author of the *Problems*) does see them as similar colors: lakes are whiter than seas or rivers, he says, and as support mentions that painters paint rivers as pale and seas as blue (*Problems* 23.6.932a27–32).

If *Problems,* book 38—which deals with skin color—is by Aristotle (or at least Aristotelian), then it is helpful here. The author appears to use λευκόν when discussing how fair (as opposed to dark) skin is, especially in connection to the effect of the sun on skin color. He does not use ὠχρός in this book of the *Problems,* but he does use related words—ἄχροος/ ἄχρους (LSJ: colorless, ill-complexioned, pallid) and εὔχροος/εὔχρους (LSJ: healthy, good complexion)—when discussing skin color in the context of health and exertion (e.g., 3.966b35). Elsewhere in the *Problems* he says that the faces of those who are afraid become pale (ὠχρόν) (27.8.948b17), and the author of the *Magna moralia* associates being pale (ὠχρὸν) with having a fever (2.10.1208a23–26).

In the authentic works, Aristotle uses ὠχρός in similar contexts. In the *Prior Analytics,* he provides the following as an example of a certain kind of improper inference: pregnant women are pale (ὠχρά), this woman is pale, therefore this woman is pregnant (2.27.70a36–37). In *HA* 2.11, he says that dying chameleons become pale (ὠχρὸς) (503b9–10).

My alternative interpretation is this: in the passage quoted at the outset of this section, Aristotle is not speaking (simply) of how dark or how white (i.e., fair skinned) women are compared to men (and females of other kinds) owing to exposure to the sun (which he must have known about).[14] Instead, he is referring to something he actually observed among Greeks, namely, that women tended to have a paler and less healthy complexion than men. He concluded that a paler complexion was part of a woman's nature and sought to explain it as best he could (knowing that what he was describing was something other than differences in skin color caused by the sun). And the reason Aristotle gives—the quantity of menses discharged—may not be irrelevant here, since a normal side effect of menstruation is anemia, which can have an effect on the pallor of the skin.

What would be the explanation for his coming to this conclusion? Well, as with the other interpretation, it could be (at least in part) the result of bias, in that he could have taken the way things were among some Greek women to be the way things were for women by nature. But I think it is at least possible that Aristotle was commenting on a less healthy complexion on the part of women, which was perhaps connected to their less healthy diet (which I discuss in the next section) and was probably related to women tending to be cooped up inside most of the time and getting little exercise. If this interpretation is correct, then Aristotle would be—in this admittedly minor passage—showing an awareness of a difference (though not of its cause) between men and women that many Greeks assumed was a difference between how men and women ought to look.

SOFTER BONES

In *PA* 2.9, Aristotle writes that "for animals that are large, there is need of supports which are stronger, larger and harder, especially for those among them that are more predatory. For this reason the bones of the males are harder than those of the females, especially those of the carnivores . . . , such as the lion" (655a10–14).

Judging by his remarks in two lengthy discussions of bones—*PA* 2.9 and *HA* 3.7—Aristotle made extensive observations of the bones of a number of kinds of animals.[15] In some cases (e.g., the lion) his observations may

14. See *Problems* 38.1, 3, 6–8, 11.
15. See also his observations in two discussions of marrow: *PA* 2.6 and *HA* 3.20.

have been aided by dissection.[16] Aristotle observed differences between the bones possessed by different kinds of animals, but nowhere does he indicate that these observations themselves led him to conclude that males have harder bones than females.

Was this claim simply the result of an inference from the principle that females are inferior to males? I don't think so. It is more likely that if it is not the result of some kind of observation, then it comes from the inference he suggests: larger animals need harder supports (bones, in the case of viviparous animals); males on the whole are larger than females; therefore, males have harder bones than females.[17]

But as Aristotle was aware, deduction of this sort did not make for the best biology. Could Aristotle have gathered any direct observational support for the claim that females had softer bones? I think he could have—at least in the case of women. As a prelude to answering this question more fully, I need to look very briefly at diet and health in the ancient Greek world.

There are a number of gaps in our knowledge of the health and diet of men and women in the ancient world, but some information is available.[18] First, although there was not often widespread famine, it is likely that food shortages were regular occurrences.[19] Further, it is likely that the poor among ancient Greeks in the classical period ate rather little meat and not too much dairy, their diet instead consisting mainly of cereals, beans, and some fish.[20] Although much remains unclear, it is likely that many ancient Greeks were malnourished and that their diets were deficient in (among other things) vitamins C and D.[21] Vitamin C deficiency can cause scurvy (which affects the development of bones and teeth), and vitamin D deficiency can cause "rickets (in infants, children), osteomalacia (in adults, especially pregnant and lactating women), osteoporosis (the elderly). There is cessation of bone growth, softening of existing bone, deformation. The cause may be dietary" (Garnsey 1989c, 33).

---

16. *PA* 2.6.651b37–652a2, 2.9.655a14; *HA* 3.7.516b7–11, 3.20.521b12–16.

17. Aristotle is also arguing that predatory animals need harder supports because they obtain their food through fighting, and thus they (are larger and therefore) need harder supports. Aristotle is wrong, of course, in implying that the female lion is not a predator.

18. On the dearth of our knowledge on this subject, see Garnsey (1999, 28, 43–44, 54).

19. See Garnsey 1988; 1999, chap. 3.

20. See Garnsey 1989a; 1989c; 1999, 13–19, 36–41, 116–27. Compare Brothwell and Brothwell 1969, 50–52.

21. On malnourishment, see Garnsey (1999, chap. 4). On deficiency diseases, see 45–48.

Peter Garnsey points out that the most vulnerable groups in times of famine and food shortages are infants and children. Women, he writes, are "the second peculiarly vulnerable group in terms of health in the third world, surely also in antiquity" (1989b, 67). Similarly, Sarah Currie writes that "a combination of poverty, manual labor and inadequate diet must have been dramatically inscribed upon the majority of women's bodies in the ancient world" (1989, 6).[22] Especially vulnerable were pregnant and lactating women (Garnsey 1999, 21, 49, 106–8).

To return to the question of whether Aristotle could have gathered any direct observational support for his claim that females (and specifically women) had softer bones, I offer as speculation that if he examined any women, then some of them likely had osteoporosis or osteomalacia.[23] This becomes quite plausible if in fact women tended to have a worse diet (and specifically, a more calcium-deficient diet) than men and/or if Aristotle (and Greeks at the time generally) observed a greater number of bone problems in older women than in older men. (Postmenopausal osteoporosis is one of the most common types; see Isselbacher et al. [1980, 1852]).[24]

As presented, his claim that females have softer bones than males is not Aristotle's biology at its best; however, it does not necessarily depend on ideologically slanted premises. It may have been the product of a wholly

---

22. On women getting less food than men, see also Garnsey (1999, 41– 42, 61, 101–3, 106– 8, 111–12).

23. Isselbacher et al. write:

Osteoporosis is the term used to describe a group of diseases . . . which are characterized by a reduction in the mass of bone per unit volume to a level below that required for adequate mechanical support function. . . . Fractures of long bones are . . . somewhat more frequent in osteoporotic subjects than in others of similar age without osteoporosis and are most common in the hip, humerus, and wrists. . . . In [some osteoporosis] patients there are suggestions of a specific defect in calcium absorption or a failure to adapt adequately to a low-calcium diet. . . .

The terms *rickets* and *osteomalacia* are used to describe a group of disorders in which there is defective mineralization of the newly formed organic matrix of the skeleton. In *rickets* the growing skeleton is involved. . . . The term *osteomalacia* is usually reserved for the disorder of mineralization of the adult skeleton. There are a number of conditions that result in rickets and/or osteomalacia such as inadequate dietary intake of vitamin D. . . . Major symptoms [of osteomalacia], when they occur, include varying degrees of diffuse skeletal pain and bony tenderness. . . . Fractures of involved bones may occur with minimal trauma. (1980, 1849, 1850, 1852, 1854, 1856)

24. Osteoporosis is more likely to occur in eunuchoid men than in normal men (see Dorfman and Shipley 1956, 315), and as discussed in the previous chapter, Aristotle saw an analogy between eunuchs and women. This could have been a reason (though hardly a conclusive one) in support of his conclusion that females have softer bones than males.

unbiased inference connecting the strength of bone to the size of the animal, and in the case of women, it may in fact have been the product of empirical observation and investigation.[25]

In *HA* 2.3, Aristotle makes one of his most infamous claims: "In the case of humans, sheep, goats and pigs, males have more teeth than females. In the case of other animals, observations have not been made" (501b19–21).

Eva Keuls comments: "Among the instances of Aristotle's misogyny parading as science, the nadir is his statement that women have fewer teeth than men" (1993, 145). Bertrand Russell, too, was unimpressed:

> Aristotle could have avoided the mistake of thinking that women have fewer teeth than men, by the simple device of asking Mrs. Aristotle to keep her mouth open while he counted. He did not do so because he thought he knew. Thinking that you know when in fact you don't is a fatal mistake, to which we are all prone. I believe myself that hedgehogs eat black beetles, because I have been told that they do; but if I were writing a book on the habits of hedgehogs, I should not commit myself until I had seen one enjoying this unappetizing dish. Aristotle, however, was less cautious. (1950, 135–36)

Note that Russell, with breathtaking arrogance, asserts what he could not possibly have known—in the process of urging us to avoid thinking we know what we don't—namely, what Aristotle did or did not do to arrive at his conclusion about the number of teeth in males and females.

Let us avoid Russell's error and instead ask whether there is any evidence that Aristotle may have relied on observation in coming to his conclusion that females had fewer teeth.[26] To begin with, judging from the *HA* 2.3 passage, he did make observations of four kinds of animals. Further, Georg Harig and Jutta Kollesch, who take a more reasonable approach to Aristotle's claim than Russell, argue that we should not conclude too quickly that there were "psychologischen Motivationen" behind Aristotle's remark about teeth. Rather, Aristotle may have arrived at his view that females have fewer teeth, they speculate, as a result of insufficient anatomical knowledge (1977, 125). They suggest three possibilities that may have led

25. Of course, it is possible that Aristotle moved—improperly—from observations about the bones of women to claims about the softness of the bones of females generally.

26. Ogle thought this line was an interpolation (1882, xiii; 88–89 of app. A, this chap.).

Aristotle to this (false) conclusion: (1) he happened to come across female animals with an anomalous number of teeth; (2) he compared animals of different ages; and (3) he examined only one woman, and she happened to lack wisdom teeth.[27] Let us consider these possibilities (in reverse order).

Point 3 is implausible because in *HA* 2.4 Aristotle reports: "The last [teeth] to grow in humans are the molars called wisdom teeth, which come at around the age of twenty years in both men and women. In some women of eighty years old, molars have grown in at the ends [of the jaws], producing great pain in coming in, and the same occurs in men too. This happens in those whose wisdom teeth did not come in at a younger age" (501b24–29). It certainly sounds as if Aristotle observed (or collected anecdotal evidence on) at least a few men and women. Moreover, it also seems he would have been aware of the possibility of the lack of wisdom teeth in any subject he was examining.

Possibility 2 seems a good (though limited) candidate for explaining Aristotle's claim in the case of nonhumans. For example, here are the number of teeth a sheep acquires throughout its life:

lamb	four pairs of incisors
1 year	middle pair of incisors
2 years	second pair of permanent incisors
3 years	third pair of permanent incisors
4 years	fourth pair of permanent incisors
5 years	all permanent incisors close together
6 years	incisors begin spreading apart
7–8 years	some incisors broken
10–12 years	all incisors missing[28]

27. Harig and Kollesch (1977, 125). I quote the important passage in full:
Oder wenn er [i.e., R. Lenoble], nur weil sich bei Aristoteles die Mitteilung findet, bei den Menschen (ebenso aber auch bei Schafen, Ziegen und Schweinen) hätten die männlichen Individuen mehr Zähne als die weiblichen, die Wissenschaftlichkeit von dessen Untersuchungen grundsätzlich in Frage stellt und die Erklärung speziell für die genannte Behauptung in psychologischen Motivationen sucht statt in ungenügenden anatomischen Kentnissen. Denn immerhin ist es nicht ausgeschlossen, daß Aristoteles (oder sein Gewährsmann in dieser Frage) deswegen von der unterschiedlichen Zahl der Zähne bei den beiden Geschlechtern überzeugt war, weil er bei seinen Recherchen zufällig auf weibliche Tiere mit Gebißanomalien stieß Tiere verschiedenen Alters miteinander verglich oder aber eine Frau untersuchte, bei der zufällig die Weisheitszähne fehlten.
In regards to an anomalous number of teeth, cf. Dean-Jones (1994, 82): "It is conceivable that, by sheer coincidence, in all the mouths he examined the male had lost fewer teeth than the female."
28. See Claeys and Rogers 2003.

(The same sort of information could be given for goats and pigs.)[29] If Aristotle had compared, say, only lambs and very old sheep, we could chastise him for having made shoddy observations. But what about subtler differences? If he did not know of the differences in the number of teeth among sheep of two, three, and four years, for example, that could have thrown off his comparison of the number of teeth in males and females. Should Aristotle have known of such differences? Perhaps. But it is hardly obvious that his not knowing must have been a result of ideologically motivated carelessness.

The problem is that this attempt to defend Aristotle is limited in that it would have been pure chance that the male sheep had more teeth than the female, and it strains belief to think that this happened, by chance, for all three nonhuman animal kinds. So I don't think possibility 2 saves Aristotle completely in the case of goats, sheep, and pigs, though this possibility may have contributed to the inaccuracy of his observations and thus his claim.

What about the possibility that Aristotle compared humans of different ages? In *Pol.* 7.16, he argues that the proper age for marriage is eighteen for women and thirty-seven or so for men (1335a7–35). (This is evidence of epistemological conservatism, since what Aristotle says reflects common ancient Greek marriage practices.) One could speculate that Aristotle compared a woman of eighteen with a man in his midthirties, though it's unclear to me why he would deliberately follow this procedure. Also, it must have been the case, in those days, that the older you were, the greater your chance of having lost teeth; so comparing teenage women to men in their midthirties might well have led Aristotle to conclude that men had fewer teeth than women. Further, as we saw earlier (in the *HA* 2.4 passage), Aristotle would have been aware of why wisdom teeth were present in a thirty-seven-year-old man but absent in an eighteen-year-old woman, so it is unlikely he would have used a comparison of men and women of these ages to support his view that males have more teeth than females.

Point 1 is more plausible but still somewhat problematic. True, Aristotle could have observed only a few subjects, all (or nearly all) of whom happened to have had an anomalous number of teeth. But since all four animals that he remarks on are common, it especially counts against him if he observed too few kinds to come to an accurate conclusion. This point is less problematic in the case of humans, for one shudders at the thought

29. See Fias Co. Farm 1997–2003 and Provet 1999–2002. My thanks to Paul Blair for bringing these two references and the one in n. 28 to my attention.

of dental hygiene in fourth century B.C. Greece. Along these lines (and similar in spirit to my suggestion in the previous section), Dean-Jones writes: "It may not have been so much of a coincidence if men had a consistently superior diet and women had lost more teeth owing to calcium deficiency in pregnancy" (1994, 82n136).[30] However, the Hippocratic text *Epidemics* (4.19, 52), of which Aristotle was most likely aware, implies that men and women have the same number of teeth. The presence of such *endoxa* ought to have made Aristotle especially careful about the nature and abundance of evidence he collected in support of his conclusion about teeth in men and women.

Nevertheless, it is likely that Aristotle made some kinds of observations about the number of teeth in males and females and that two of the three possibilities offered by Harig and Kollesch go some way to possibly explaining why Aristotle's observations—without being tainted by ideology—did not lead him to the truth.

Aside from direct observation, what sort of argument might Aristotle have made in support of his position that males had more teeth than females? In the *Parts of Animals,* he writes:

> Of the instrumental parts that are for defense and protection, nature provides each of them only, or especially, to those animals that are able to use them, and especially to the animals able to use them most—parts such as sting, spur, horns, tusks, and any other such part there may be. And since the male is stronger and more spirited, in some cases he alone has such parts, in other cases he more than the female. For those parts which it is necessary for females to have as well, e.g., parts related to nourishment, they have, but they have less; while those related to none of the necessities, they do not have. (3.1.661b28–662a2; see also *GA* 5.8.788b3–6)

Aristotle may have applied this general "doctrine" to the case of human teeth—a case about which he concluded the evidence was sketchy and inconclusive. However, he could not have consistently applied this passage to the number of teeth in humans. Aristotle says in that passage that, among animals that have teeth for nourishment as well as for defense and protection, males will have the parts related to nourishment to a greater de-

---

30. There is a longstanding myth that "a woman loses a tooth for every child she has," and like many myths, it may have some basis in fact. (I came across this line in two dentistry Web sites: http://members.rediff.com/drkhosla/pregnancy.html and http://home.istar.ca/~sjr/Clinical/pregnancy.htm. John Steinbeck's 1952 novel *East of Eden,* pt. 2, chap. 17, sec. 1, has: "A woman gave a tooth for a child.")

gree. But humans do not fall into this class of animal, as the rest of *PA* 3.1 makes clear (see also 2.9.655b8–11). So if Aristotle did apply this passage to the issue of the number of teeth in men and women, then Lloyd is right to suggest the possibility that Aristotle was "misled by the doctrine that males have the parts of nutrition 'to a greater degree' than females" (1983, 102).[31]

An even less likely application of a principle to explain the claim that men have fewer teeth than women is suggested by *Problems* 34.1: "Why is it that those who have widely spaced teeth are not long lived? Is it because the long lived have more teeth, for instance males have more than females, men than women, and rams than ewes? Those men who have widely spaced teeth apparently resemble those who have fewer teeth" (963b18–22). I suppose it is just possible that Aristotle arrived at a certain generalization (more teeth, longer life), added to it the fact (as he saw it) that males tend to live longer than females (see *On Length and Shortness of Life* 5.466b9–17), and concluded—in part based on this deduction, in part based on observation—that men have more teeth than women. But I think Aristotle would have followed such a procedure only in the absence of sufficient direct evidence about the relative number of teeth in males and females (men and women); and even so, there is no evidence that he did so.

Whatever use Aristotle might have made of these two principles—that the parts for nutrition exist to a greater degree in males and that an animal with more teeth tends to live longer—I think James Lennox is right to "note how strange it would be *not* to have based [his conclusion about males having more teeth] on observation, given Aristotle's explicit refusal to generalize a priori" (1985, 320).[32]

In conclusion to this section, let us apply the test for ideological rationalization. First, does Aristotle's claim that males have more teeth than females tend to justify gender prejudice? As Lennox asks, "What would be at stake for a male-dominant ideology here?" (1985, 320). I don't think there is much that one can come up with. One might appeal to *GA* 5.8, where Aristotle writes that "the existence [of teeth] is not for one purpose only, nor do they exist for the same purpose in all animals: some have teeth on account of nourishment, some for self-defense and some for reasoning with voice" (788b4–5). But Aristotle never says (and this would be bizarre indeed) that the fewer the teeth a human has, the less his or her capacity for reasoning!

31. See also Dean-Jones 1994, 81n134.
32. Lennox refers to *GA* 3.10.760b27–33, quoted above in chaps. 1 and 2, 13, 24.

Of course, one might argue that any false claim about the superiority—even the physical superiority—of males to females would contribute to gender prejudice. I think this is false but nevertheless proceed to the second part of the test: Is Aristotle's claim about the number of teeth in males and females supported by arbitrary assumptions and/or unusually bad arguments? I don't think so. Although there is some chance that he applied principles a priori, I find it highly unlikely that this is the sole explanation for his views about teeth or that such an application of principles must have been arbitrary or ideologically motivated. Aristotle probably engaged in some kind of observations on this matter; and, there are some plausible hypotheses about what observations may have led him, without contradiction, to this false conclusion about teeth.

So, we should not follow Russell, Nussbaum, Keuls, and a host of others and conclude that Aristotle said stupid things about the number of teeth in females without looking (to paraphrase Nussbaum). When considered in the broader context of his biology, it becomes highly unlikely that Aristotle simply assigned women fewer teeth because he was a misogynist.

Further, I submit that the application of the test for ideological rationalization to the other claims of Aristotle discussed in this chapter—with the possible exception of his remarks about women having paler skin—would yield similar results, that is, that they were not the result of bias. True, the explanations on Aristotle's behalf in this chapter are very speculative. So in evaluating his biology, it counts against him that—at least in the cases discussed in this chapter—he gave us so little information about the observations and/or arguments that led him to his conclusions. Nevertheless, there is little basis for the view that Aristotle arrived at the conclusions he did by the arbitrary application of sexist principles, with no concern for observation. The most we can plausibly say is that Aristotle's expectation that females would be physically inferior to males in areas not yet researched (because females tend to be inferior in height, combative weapons, strength, etc.) possibly caused him to investigate these matters insufficiently. But we should not conclude that his remarks are therefore "misogynist and silly."

APPENDIX A: AN EXCERPT FROM OGLE (1882, XI–XIII)

A few words on . . . [Aristotle's] supposed inaccuracy of observation. I cannot but think that this has been, to say the least, enormously exaggerated. Were we indeed to suppose that Aristotle had committed all the extravagant blunders which critics have laid to his charge, the accusation would have to be admitted as just. But a very large proportion, at any rate, of his supposed mistakes have no other ground than the careless mode in which his writings have been studied. They are not mistakes of Aristotle, but mistakes of his critics. To give a few examples. It is laid to his charge that he represented the arteries as void of blood and containing nothing but air; the aorta as springing from the right ventricle; the heart as beating in man and in no other animal, and as not liable to disease; the gall bladder as situated in some animals on or close to the tail; reptiles as having no blood; and so on, till the list might be swollen with almost every conceivable absurdity. In reality not one of the errors here enumerated was made by him. Still I am far from denying that there are strange misstatements of simple facts to be found in his works. That there is but a single bone in the neck of the lion and of the wolf; that there are more teeth in male than in female animals; that the mouth of the dolphin is placed, as in rays and sharks, on the under surface of the body; these and the like are strange blunders, however they originated. This much, however, seems to me beyond question: these were not the personal observations of the same man who had noted the heart beating in the embryonic chick as a "punctum saliens" on the third day of incubation; who had distinguished the allantoidean development of birds and reptiles from the nonallantoidean development of fishes; who had unravelled with fair accuracy the arrangement of the bronchial tubes and their relation to the pulmonary blood vessels; and who had not only given zoological and anatomical details concerning the cephalopods, which both Cuvier and Owen regard as "truly astonishing," but had described nine species of them "with so much precision and happy a selection of their distinctive characters as to enable modern naturalists to identify pretty nearly all."[33]

Is it possible to believe that the same eye that had distinguished the cetacea from the fishes, that had detected their hidden mammæ, discovered their lungs, and recognized the distinct character of their bones, should have been so blind as to fancy that the mouth of these animals was on the under surface of the body? Although a statement to this effect occurs twice over in the Greek text, yet it is to me as incredible that it should have been actually made by Aristotle, as it would be that Professor Huxley should make a similar palpable misstatement about an animal with which

33. In a footnote at this point, Ogle cites "Todd's Cycopedia, i. 561." (Here, as elsewhere, he gives no fuller bibliographical information.)

he was perfectly familiar. If it be asked how we can account for the presence of the erroneous statement in the text, we have not to go far for, at any rate, a very possible explanation. We have only to remember the strange vicissitudes to which the original manuscripts of Aristotle's treatises are said to have been subjected. Hidden underground in the little town of Scepsis, to save them from the hands of the kings of Peramus, who were then collecting books to form their famous library, and who, in doing so, apparently paid but little regard to their rights of individual owners, they were left for the better part of two centuries to moulder in the damp, "blattarum et tinearum epulæ;" and when they were at last again brought to light, fell into the hands of Apellicon of Teos, a man who, Strabo says, was a lover of books rather than a philosopher, and who felt no scruples in correcting what had become worm eaten, and supplying what was defective or illegible.[34] To what extent this corruption of the very fountain head took place, we have now absolutely no means whatsoever of ascertaining. We are, however, I think, justified in assuming with much confidence that such palpable absurdities as the one which has just been mentioned were due to this sacrilegious interference with the text, and should be put not to the account of Aristotle, but to that of the incompetent Apellicon, or his fellow transcribers and emendators. Similarly would I explain another blunder already mentioned, namely, the statement which occurs in the Historia Animalium, that in certain species of animals, namely men goat sheep and swine, the teeth are more numerous in the males than in the females, a blunder which has been quoted, with others, by Mr. Lewes, as an instance of Aristotle's carelessness in observation.[35] That this statement is due to interpolation or correction of the original manuscript I feel the more assured, because in other passages, in the De Partibus, when the distinctions between males and females as regards their horns, teeth, and their offensive and defensive weapons generally, are discussed, no such erroneous statement is to be found.[36] It is said, and said correctly, that horns and tusks are often larger in the male than in the female, and horns frequently wanting in the latter when present in the former; but as to any difference in the number of teeth, there is not a single word. We can readily conceive how an incompetent editor, finding in the manuscript a half legible passage relating to the teeth of male and female animals, may have so filled up the gap as to convert a difference of size into

34. In a footnote at this point, Ogle cites "Grote's Aristotle, i. 51" (Grote 1883).
35. Lewes (1864).
36. In a footnote at this point, Ogle cites PA 3.1.

a difference of number. Some of the more striking blunders in Aristotle's treatises, especially such as occur only in single instances, may, I think, be fairly thus explained.

APPENDIX B: MENSTRUATING WOMEN, THE WANING OF THE MOON, AND BLOODY MIRRORS

Since this chapter discusses Aristotle's more bizarre remarks about women, I would be remiss if I did not mention a couple of strange passages on menstruation (the second of which being perhaps his most bizarre remark of all). But because these are not (as the others in this chapter are) about the differences between the parts of males and females, I have placed this brief mention of them in an appendix.

In *GA* 4.2, Aristotle writes: "Also the fact that the menstrual discharge in the natural course tends to take place when the moon is waning is due to the same cause. That time of month is colder and more fluid on account of the waning and failure of the moon" (767a2–6).[37] So Aristotle is claiming: that women tend to have menstrual cycles of the same length, occurring at the same time; that these menstrual cycles correspond to the length of the lunar cycle; and that the lunar cycle causes or controls the menstrual cycle. None of these claims is true.[38] Dean-Jones suggests how Aristotle (and other ancients) might have obtained some evidence for the first of these claims:

> Now, the ideal for a respectable Athenian man of the Classical period was to be wealthy enough to have no need for his women to leave the home, and there is some modern evidence that women who live in close quarters with each other, especially if they are confined and their day is controlled largely by artificial light, can become synchronized in their menstrual cycles.[39] It is therefore conceivable that the wife, concubine, daughters, and female slaves of many families did menstruate at about the same time, and as it is unlikely that the average Greek man inquired into the menstrual cycle of households other than his own this may have given support to the belief that all women menstruated at the same time. But even if

37. Translation from Dean-Jones 1994, 97. Balme (1991, 425) writes that the wane of the moon "is the last eight days before the new moon at which each month theoretically began." For a somewhat different account by Aristotle of menstruation and the waning of the moon, see *HA* 9 (7).2.582b-3–4 (and Dean-Jones 1994, 96n181).

38. See Dean-Jones 1994, 94.

39. Dean-Jones here cites Asso (1983, 7).

we allow that women within a household became synchronized in their menstruation, this is not sufficient to explain the further notion that menstruation tended to coincide with the waning moon. (1994, 97)

Aristotle had on hand a theory (about the effects of hot and cold on the state of blood) that could explain a supposed connection between the lunar and menstrual cycles. It seems that this caused him to move too hastily from "women tend to have menstrual cycles of the same length" to "their menstrual cycles occur at the same time, and correspond to the waning of the moon." If so, Aristotle allowed the standard outlook of the culture on this issue to lead him to a conclusion beyond what the evidence supported. However, I think it unlikely that such carelessness is an indication of ideological bias. What social interest or political agenda could a connection between menstruation and the lunar cycle support?

Aristotle's *On Dreams*, book 2, contains the following infamous passage:

> That the sense organs are acutely sensitive to even a slight qualitative difference is shown by what happens in the case of mirrors; a subject to which, even taking it independently, one might devote close consideration and inquiry. At the same time it becomes plain from them that as the eye is affected, so also it produces a certain effect. For in the case of very bright mirrors, when women during their menstrual periods look into the mirror, the surface of the mirror becomes a sort of bloodshot cloud; and if the mirror is new, it is not easy to wipe off such a stain, while if it is old it is easier. The cause is, as we said, that the eye is not only affected by the air but also has an effect upon it and moves it. (459b23–460a3)[40]

There are connected debates about the authenticity of this passage and about how well it fits into its broader context in *On Dreams*, book 2.[41] I certainly cannot enter into these debates here, though I am inclined to agree with David Gallop that "it is hard to believe that Aristotle gave any credence to such old wives' tales. Nothing of the sort is ever suggested in the scientific accounts of menstruation given in his zoological treatises" (1996, 145).[42]

---

40. This is the translation in the rev. Oxford trans. of Aristotle. I assume it is the translation of the editor, Jonathan Barnes (1984b), because the original Oxford translation rendered this passage into Latin.

41. On the authenticity of the passage, see Ross (1955, 272–73). On how well it fits into its context in *On Dreams*, bk. 2, see Sprague (1985) and Gallop (1996, 145–46).

42. See also Dean-Jones 1994, 229–30.

I do not know what to make of this passage. Obviously, Aristotle (if he is the author) did not conclude what he did as a result of observation. If authentic, *On Dreams* 2.59b23–460a3 shows that Aristotle sometimes accepted as anecdotal evidence accounts that he ought to have rejected. This passage is embarrassing but not because of what it says about Aristotle's conception of women. For it is neither a claim about any alleged inferiority of women nor is it evidence for the idea that Aristotle engaged in ideological rationalization in coming to his conclusions about women. I can think of nothing—ideological or otherwise—that would have led Aristotle to come to this conclusion.

| THE SOFTER AND LESS SPIRITED SEX

In an important passage in the *History of Animals,* Aristotle presents, in some detail, differences in character and cognition between the male and the female. What precisely are his views on these issues? What are the sources of his views? And are they connected to his more infamous claims about the cognitive and character traits of women? (For example, according to Aristotle, the relationship of man and woman is that of ruler and ruled, with the woman sharing in rule only in the household, and the different functions of man and woman entail that the virtues are different for men and women. And concerning female intelligence, Aristotle claims that man is to woman as soul is to body or as reason is to appetite; the woman possesses the deliberative part of the soul, but it lacks authority; the intellectual virtues are different for men and women—most significantly, whereas men can possess practical intelligence, the most a woman can attain is true opinion.)[1] Finally, is there evidence that Aristotle's remarks in his biology on the character and cognition of males and females are the result of ideological bias?

HISTORY OF ANIMALS 8 (9).1.608A21–B18

Since *HA* 8 (9).1.608a21–b18 is the focus of this chapter, it seems worthwhile reproducing the most relevant parts of it here below.[2]

---

1. See, e.g., *Pol.* 1.13, 3.4.1277b24–29, *NE* 8.7.1158b11–28, 8.11.1161a22–25, *Rhet.* 1.5. 1361a4–10.

2. There is a dispute over the authenticity of *HA,* bks. 8–10. See Balme (1991, 1–13) for details. See also Huby (1985) on a possible Theophrastean contribution to *HA,* bk. 8 (9). I proceed on the assumption that *HA,* bk. 8 (9) is authentic, for Lloyd is right (1983, 21–24)

In all kinds [of animals] in which there are the female and the male, nature has established much the same difference in the character of the females as compared with that of the males. But it is most evident in the case of humans, larger animals, and viviparous quadrupeds. For the character of the females is softer, quicker to be tamed, more receptive to handling, and readier to learn (for example, the female Laconian dogs are in fact cleverer than the males). . . .

All females are less spirited than males, except the bear and leopard: in these the female is thought to be braver. But in the other kinds, the females are softer, more vicious, less simple, more impetuous, and more attentive to the feeding of the young, while the males, on the contrary, are more spirited, wilder, simpler, and less cunning. There are traces of these characteristics in virtually all animals, but they are all the more evident in those that have more character, and especially in the human. For the human has the most complete nature, so that these dispositions too are more evident in humans. This is why a woman is more compassionate than a man and more given to tears, but also more jealous, more complaining, more scolding, and more apt to fight. The female is also more dispirited and more despondent than the male, more shameless and more lying, readier to deceive and possessing a better memory; and further, she is more wakeful, more timid, and in general, the female is less inclined to move than the male, and requires less nourishment. But as we have said, the male is more able to help and braver than the female, since even among cephalopods, when the cuttlefish is struck by the trident, the male helps the female, whereas the female runs away when the male is struck.

Of the traits attributed to females here, two seem to have priority: that females are softer than males and that they are less spirited. These fundamental facts about females, as Aristotle sees it, seem to give rise to, or in any event are related to, two further and connected sets of female characteristics: cognitive traits and character traits. Concerning cognition, Aristotle claims that females are quicker to tame, more receptive to handling, more ready to learn, possessed of longer memories, and cleverer. As for positive character traits, Aristotle says that females are more compassionate than males, more attentive to the young, and more wakeful or vigilant. On the negative side, he makes the following points:

---

that even if it is not by Aristotle, *HA*, bk. 8 (9), is Aristotelian: it fits into his program and with what he says in other works.

1. general inferiority: females are more vicious and shameless;
2. insufficient control of emotions: females are prone to tears, jealous, and impetuous and are more likely to complain, scold, and fight;
3. cowardice: females are less brave and so are more afraid of action and less inclined to move (and thus make poor allies);
4. deception: females are bigger liars, more ready to deceive, less straightforward, and more cunning.

In this chapter, I focus on Aristotle's claim that females are softer (μαλακώτερα) and less spirited (ἀθυμότερα) before covering some of his other, derivative claims about female character traits. But first, let me treat his remarks about female cognition, which at first glance come across as relatively positive.

FEMALE COGNITION

A full discussion of Aristotle's claims about female intellectual capabilities is beyond the scope of this work, which focuses on the biological writings. For in the opening chapter of *Parts of Animals,* Aristotle writes that in a sense, "it will be requisite for the person studying nature to speak about soul more than the matter, inasmuch as it is more that the matter is nature because of soul than the reverse." But he adds that in light of this, "one might puzzle over whether it is up to natural science to speak about *all* soul, or some part, since if it speaks about all, no philosophy is left besides natural science. This is because reason [νοῦς] is of the objects of reason, so that natural science would be knowledge about everything. For it is up to the same science to study reason and its objects" (641a32–b2). So, Aristotle is quite explicit that the study of reason and thought are outside the scope of biology. And as James Lennox argues (1999b), this is a limitation that Aristotle follows in his biology. Aristotle may discuss the cognitive functions and attributes of some animals—as he does in *HA* 8 (9).1—but he does not discuss the human intellect per se or compare the intellect of other animals to the human intellect.

So what is Aristotle saying in our *HA* 8 (9).1 passage? He makes a number of claims about female cognition that, out of context, sound like praise and, thus, may be taken as evidence for something better than what is suggested by the infamous claims mentioned at the outset of this chapter. For he seems to be saying that females are cleverer, more ready to learn, and have better memories (608a25–28, b13).[3] But taken in context, I believe this passage does not paint a positive picture of female cognition.

First, Aristotle says that "the character of the females is softer, quicker to be tamed, more receptive of handling, and readier to learn (for example, the female Laconian dogs are in fact cleverer than the males)" (608a25–28). He is here discussing the domestication, taming, and handling of animals. In that context, he says that females are "better"—that is, easier to tame and train—than males. This explains why he says that males are "wilder" (ἀγριώτερα) than females (608b3). Further, the passage begins with a reference to the female's softness and is located in a context that makes much of the female's lower level of spiritedness. This is significant: less-spirited animals are easier to control, and softer animals need to be controlled.[4]

What are the implications here for women? Aristotle says in HA 8 (9).1 that "there are traces of these characteristics in virtually all animals, but they are all the more evident in those that have more character, and especially in the human" (608b4–6). Certainly, we should not conclude that HA 8 (9).1.608a25–28 implies that women are simply smarter than men— that they would, for example, be better equipped to study science or philosophy—for this passage says nothing one way or another about such high-level cognitive functions: it is not discussing human intelligence per se but lower-level cognitive traits found in (some) animals and, to some degree, in humans.

I believe these claims about the "handling" of females—and Aristotle's willingness to extend them to women—imply that one would have greater success training a woman to run a household (to do domestic work) than one would training a (nonslave) man.[5] As such, this passage is at the very least consistent with the infamous claims about female cognition mentioned above.

What about his claim that females possess better memories than males? Here it is in its context: "The female is also more dispirited and more despondent than the male, more shameless and more lying, readier to deceive and possessing a better memory [μνημονικώτερον]" (608b11–

---

3. One may be tempted to add to the list Aristotle's claim that males are "less cunning" than females (as Balme [1991] translates it, 608b4), but this would clearly be a mistake. As I demonstrate below, what Aristotle is in fact saying is that women are more scheming or plotting than males, which makes this an instance of her supposedly greater dishonesty.

4. See HA 1.1.488b12–15.

5. On just such training of women, see Xenophon's Oeconomica.

13). Μνημονικός certainly can mean "having a good memory" (LSJ, s.v. μνημονικός), and we must remain open to the possibility that that is precisely what Aristotle is attributing to females (including women). But given the full passage within which the claim is made, Balme is right in translating μνημονικώτερον as "has a longer memory" (1991, 219), especially if he means to connote that Aristotle is saying that females are petty and thus more likely to hold a grudge or not forget a perceived slight. But even if the more positive reading is what Aristotle intended, it is difficult to escape the conclusion—given what was said earlier in the *HA* 8 (9).1 passage—that this better memory is connected to the female's superior ability to be domesticated.

Aristotle's claims about female cognition are connected to his claims about female character and, especially, his view that females are softer and less spirited than males. Further, as I hope will become clear, I think they ultimately have the same source as his claims about female character, namely, a combination of observations of domesticated and wild animals, observations of the women he came into contact with, and the popular opinions and literary tradition with which he was familiar. Therefore, in what follows, I concentrate on Aristotle's remarks about female character.

NATURAL VIRTUE AND VIRTUE IN THE STRICT SENSE

It is crucial to limit the focus of our discussion to Aristotle's remarks on character in his biological writings, for what he says there is not—or at least not directly—connected to his claims about human virtue in his ethical writings. Let me explain.

Lennox, in "Aristotle on the Biological Roots of Virtue: The Natural History of Natural Virtue" (1999a), reminds us of the distinction Aristotle makes in the *Nicomachean Ethics* between natural virtues—found in beasts and children—and virtue in the strict sense, which is found in (certain) adult humans and requires deliberation, choice, and practical intelligence (φρόνησις). (See *NE* 6.7.1144b1–16.) Lennox writes:

> How . . . can [Aristotle] ascribe both natural virtue and practical intelligence to other animals and yet deny them the unqualified virtue that comes to us when we have both? The answer, supported by Aristotle's account of animal character in *HA* VII–VIII, lies in the *independence* of the cognitive capacities and character traits in other animals, and thus in the fact that animals act "in character" without deliberative choice. The other animals do not need to integrate practical intelligence with natural virtues

to achieve excellence of character—in humans, however, it is this very integration that is the essence of both practical intelligence and virtuous character. (1999a, 12–13)

I believe that in the course of the article Lennox successfully defends this position and, further, the view that, according to Aristotle, "humans begin life with the very *natural capacities* that are the beast's *likenesses* of bravery, temperance, understanding, or intelligence, yet end up with quite different *learned and acquired states,* namely *true* bravery and intelligence" (1999a, 18).[6]

The importance of all of this, for the present chapter, is that Aristotle, in the above *HA* 8 (9).1 passage, is discussing the natural character traits of certain animals (including humans)—not virtues in the strict sense, which are not found in nonhuman animals. Therefore, virtue is beyond the scope of biology and, thus, of this present study (just as reason and thought are, as we have seen). When Aristotle speaks in the biology of bravery, cowardice, spiritedness, softness, and the rest, he does not have in mind states of character that result from deliberation and choice but, rather, the analogue (or precursor) of those states, which are found in human beings alone.[7]

I turn now to Aristotle's claims about the softness and spiritedness of males and females. Although I shall make use of his relevant discussions in the ethical writings, I shall abide by the limitations just described and rely solely on passages that—or insofar as they—shed light on what Aristotle says about character traits that can be possessed by animals.

According to Aristotle, there are three kinds of desire (ὄρεξις): wish (βούλησις), spirit (θυμός), and appetite (ἐπιθυμία) (*DA* 2.1.412b2, *De motu animalium* 6.700b22). Wish is rational desire; appetite and spirit reside in the nonrational part of the soul (*DA* 3.9.432b6), though in the case of humans both can be mastered by reason.[8] (Wish or rational desire applies only to humans and, as such, will not concern us here.) In the case of appetite, Aristotle has in mind bodily pleasures and the desire to avoid bodily pains—especially those connected to food and sex. Spirit concerns or includes such emotions as anger, fear, hope for revenge, and the emo-

6. Note that as Lennox points out (1999a, 25), Aristotle never calls these natural character traits virtues.

7. So in what follows, I make use of Aristotle's ethical works only insofar as they clarify our understanding of the natural basis of the character traits described in *HA* 8 (9).1.

8. On mastering and being mastered, see *NE* 7.7; *Topics* 5.1.129a10–16. Spirit can, in a sense, obey reason (*NE* 7.6.1149a25–b2).

tional bonds of friendship.⁹ Aristotle's claim that females are softer than males concerns the appetites; his claim that females are less spirited concerns spirit.

SOFTER

Liddell, Scott, and Jones give two main senses of the term μαλαχός: (1) of things subject to touch, it means "soft" and (2) of things not subject to touch, it can mean "soft," "gentle," "fair," "tender," "mild," "faint," "delicate," "light," and in a clearly pejorative sense, "faint-hearted," "cowardly," "morally weak," "lacking in self-control." Aristotle uses μαλαχός in both senses, but what concerns us is his use of μαλαχός—which I translate as "soft" throughout—in the second sense. So, what does Aristotle mean when he says that females are softer than males?

Being soft concerns how well one handles pleasures and pains (*NE* 7.4.1147b21–23). More specifically, Aristotle sometimes says that softness refers to bodily pleasures (*NE* 7.4.1148a11–13) or matters of comfort (*Rhet.* 1.10.1368b18). But more often he speaks in terms of pain.¹⁰

In *NE* 7.7, Aristotle claims that it is possible to be defeated by those pleasures that most people master and to master those that defeat most people. He says the former is a lack of self-control, whereas the latter is the possession of it. Similarly, he claims that it is possible to withstand pain or discomfort that most people cannot withstand and to fail to withstand pain or discomfort that most people can withstand. The former condition is endurance, the latter, softness. So softness is (most of all) the inability to withstand or endure the pain and discomfort that most people could if they had to.¹¹

> Now the man who is defective in respect of resistance to the things which most people both resist and resist successfully is soft and effeminate [μαλαχὸς καὶ τρυφῶν]; for effeminacy too is a kind of softness; such a man trails his cloak to avoid the pain of lifting it, and plays the invalid without thinking himself wretched, though the man he imitates is a wretched man. . . . But it is surprising if a man is defeated by and cannot resist pleasures or pains which most men can hold out against, when this

9. See *Topics* 4.5.126a8–10; *EE* 3.1.1229b31–32; *Pol.* 7.7.1327b36–1328a7.
10. Compare Plato *Republic* 8.550b–c.
11. See *NE* 7.7.1150a9–15, 31–b5; *EE* 2.6.1202b29–36; *Rhet.* 2.6.1383b33–1384a2.

is not due to heredity or disease, like the softness that is hereditary with the kings of the Scythians, or that which distinguishes the female sex from the male.[12] (*NE* 7.7.1150b1–5, b12–16)

This description of softness is clearly taken by him to apply to men who—through poor deliberation and wrong choices—are soft, as well as to those animals (including some humans) who he believes are soft not as a result of choice but by nature (including by heredity or disease). According to Aristotle, such a state applies to females (including women) by nature.

Softness is neither a virtue nor a vice (*NE* 7.1.1145a35–b2). But for a healthy, physically normal male, it is blameworthy, as we have seen—because it depends on deliberation and choice—and such men are called effeminate (see also *NE* 7.1.1145a35–b9). But as we have also seen, for men who are effeminate by nature or disease—and for women—it is not a moral flaw to be softer than normal men. Even in the case of normal men, softness does not rule out moral worth completely. Softness involves a pretty narrow issue. For example, a person can be soft about enduring extremes of hot and cold and still be brave about death (*EE* 3.1.1229b1–8).

In sum, according to Aristotle, females by their nature are less able to endure pain and hardships and to do without certain comforts than males.

LESS SPIRITED

I turn now to female spirit. Here are three excerpts from the passage quoted from *HA* 8 (9).1 at the beginning of this chapter:

All females are less spirited [ἀθυμότερα] than males, except the bear and leopard: in these the female is thought to be braver. But in the other kinds, the females are softer, [etc.]. (608a33–b1)

Males are more spirited [θυμωδέστερα]. (608b3)

The female is more dispirited [δύσθυμον μᾶλλον]. (608b11)

So, Aristotle thought that, with a couple of kinds of exceptions, females were less spirited than males and that this characteristic is in some way connected to females being softer and less brave.[13] What does Aristotle mean in saying that females are less spirited than males?

---

12. I shall say more about these Scythians later.
13. Being highly spirited contributes to courage (*Rhet.* 2.12.1389a26–29).

According to LSJ, ἄθυμος can mean "fainthearted," "without spirit," "discouraging," "without anger or passion"; δύσθυμος can mean "dispirited," "despondent"; and θυμοειδής/θυμώδης can mean "passionate," "hot tempered," "high spirited," "fierce." Each of these is based on the more fundamental word θυμός (which, for consistency's sake, I translate as "spirit" throughout).

In an important passage from NE 3.8, we see clearly how Aristotle was able to use θυμός (and related concepts) both for those traits found in a soul by nature and for those that arise as the result of deliberation and choice. Note also the distinction between the genuine virtue, bravery, and a level of spiritedness in certain animals that can also be called "bravery," though not fully (or fully accurately).

> Spirit is also counted as bravery; for those who act from spirit—like beasts when they attack those who have wounded them—also seem to be brave, because brave people are highly spirited [θυμοειδεῖς]. Spirit is most eager to rush at dangers. . . . Brave people act for the sake of the noble, and spirit cooperates with them. But beasts act because of pain; for they attack because they have been wounded or frightened, since if they are in the forest, they do not approach us. . . . The "bravery" caused by spirit seems to be the most natural, and to *be* bravery once choice and the goal have been added to it. Human beings as well as beasts find it painful to be angered, and pleasant to exact their revenge. Those who fight for these reasons, however, are good fighters, but they are not brave; for they fight not because of what is noble or according to reason, but because of their feelings. Still, they have something similar to courage. (1116b22–1117a9)

According to Aristotle, females in some sense have a less forceful soul. They are less emotional in a certain respect—not with respect to appetites, for example, but with respect to the emotions associated with "spirit."

In HA 1.1, Aristotle says: "Animals differ in character in the following respects. Some are good tempered, dispirited (δύσθυμα), and not prone to ferocity, like the ox; others are quick-tempered, ferocious and unteachable, like the wild boar" (488b12–15).[14] At the risk of stacking the cards against Aristotle, we could say that a female, in his view, is more like an ox than a boar: she will tend to be despondent, not quick-tempered. She will not be

---

14. See also HA 7 (8).1.588a16–25.

eager to rush into danger, but would more likely seek to avoid it. Finally, females on his view are more likely to be obedient, and to be tamed and controlled.[15]

That females are less spirited, as Aristotle sees it, is no doubt connected to their being softer. For instance, he might think female spirit is too weak to beat down a woman's desire for bodily pleasures. What else can we say about her being less spirited? There is a clear connection between lack of spirit and the following traits from *HA* 8 (9).1: that females are less brave, more afraid of action, and thus less inclined to help (608a33–35, b14–18).[16]

Further, female "dishonesty" comes, at least in part, from a lack of spirit. Aristotle says that females are bigger liars, and are more ready to deceive, than males (*HA* 8 [9].1.608b12); they are also, he says, less straightforward or frank (ἧττον ἁπλᾶ) (608b1).[17] In *Rhetoric* 1.9, he says that the angry and excitable person is straightforward (1367a38). This suggests that people who act in a spirited way tend to act immediately and express exactly what they think or feel, whereas those who do not—those who lack a strong spirit and can sit back and mull something over—are more likely to make up a story, say, to get what they want.

Similarly, he says that males are less cunning or scheming (ἧττον ἐπίβουλα) than females are. Earlier in the *History of Animals*, he contrasts spiritedness (θυμοὶ) and mischievousness (πανουργίαι) (7 [8].1.588a16–25). Again, he seems to think that, for example, when a male is slighted, he is more likely to get angry and act immediately, from his spirit, whereas a female in the same situation, lacking a strong spirit, would sit back and plot and scheme. There is likely a connection between spirit and appetite here as well. In the *Nicomachean Ethics*, he writes: "A spirited man [θυμώδης] is not given to scheming [ἐπίβουλα], nor is spirit [θυμός], which is open. But the nature of appetite is illustrated by what the poets call Aphrodite,

15. See also *Pol.* 7.7.1327b23–1328a7. On spirit and control in the case of slaves, see *Pol.* 7.10.1330a25–27; *Oeconomica* 1.5.1344b13–14.

16. On spirit and courage, see Herodotus 1.37; 7.11; Thucydides 2.88; and Isocrates 3.58. But note that Aristotle also sees a connection between softness and indolence or inaction: "The lover of amusement, too, is thought to be self-indulgent, but is really soft. For amusement is a relaxation, since it is a rest; but the lover of amusement is one of the people who go to excess in this" (*NE* 7.7.1150b16–19).

17. Although ἁπλῶς generally means "simple, without qualification" in Aristotle, in the context of this passage it clearly suggests some kind of honesty, best conveyed by "frank" or "straightforward." See *EE* 3.7, where the straightforward person is the mean between the dissembler and the boaster (1236b38). I confess having a difficult time imagining what dishonesty and fraud among nonhumans (i.e., in a nonmoral sense) might mean.

'guile-weaving daughter of Cyprus'" (7.6.1149b1–18). I take it he means that women, with stronger appetites and weaker spirits, will be more likely to plot and deceive and generally be dishonest in order to fulfill their pleasures and avoid pain.

THE MORAL CHARACTER OF WOMEN

Aristotle can obviously use moral concepts when discussing nonmoral agents (i.e., nonhuman animals). This may well be a flaw in his biology, but it is not obviously an ideological one. Now he clearly held that males by nature tend to have better characters than females. What does all of this imply about his conception of woman?

For Aristotle, that women are softer and less spirited than men cannot be taken as a moral flaw—any more than a doe lacking horns could make her morally inferior to a stag.[18] But it can be taken as an indication of "psychological" inferiority: on his view, when it comes to spirit and (the soul's control over) appetite, women are weaker than men. In the realms of life involving spirit—anger, fear, revenge—women are by their nature sluggish, less able to confront or overcome their fears, less eager to exact vengeance swiftly, and less able to withstand being controlled. In the realms of life involving bodily appetites, women are by their nature more indolent and less able to resist pleasure and endure pain and discomfort.[19]

What further implications does Aristotle's conception of the woman's soul have for his view of the moral capacities of women? First, what specific claims about the moral character of women—from *HA* 8 (9).1 and the rest of the corpus—stem from his position that females are softer than males? As he sees it, that females are more impetuous (προπετέστερα [*HA* 8 (9).1.608b1–2]) than males is clearly a consequence of feminine softness, and this has implications for his view of a woman's moral capacities. Impetuousness is a kind of lack of self-control (ἀκρασία): an impetuous person deliberates about the best course of action but then fails to act on his or her conclusion because of appetite (*NE* 7.7.1150b19–21). Such a person is soft on appetites.

Aristotle maintains that girls have a stronger sexual drive and, thus, must be watched more carefully than boys (*HA* 9 [7].1.581b11–16, *Pol.* 7.16.1335a7–15; but cf. *HA* 5.8.542a30–b1), which fits perfectly his conception of their being softer than males. Further, his discussions of Spartan

---

18. On the sense in which acting from spirit is not voluntary, see *NE* 3.1.1110a25, 3.2.1111b11.
19. On being dispirited and idle, see *HA* 8 (9).40.627a33–b2.

women—and the deleterious effect they had on Sparta—suggest that he believed women in general have a greater tendency to love money and the pleasures and comforts that can be attained through its possession (*Pol.* 2.9.1269b12–1270a29, *Rhet.* 1.5.1361a9–11). His claim that females—including women—are more prone to tears (*HA* 8 [9].1.608b9) may have some connection to their purported dearth of spirit, but it is more (or more likely) connected to their softness: they more easily cry about pain and discomfort or the loss of pleasures and comforts. In the *Nicomachean Ethics,* he writes that women and womanly men are more given to mourning than are normal men (9.11.1171b6–12).

Finally, in our *HA* passage, he says that "a woman is . . . (1) more jealous, (2) more complaining, (3) more scolding, and (4) more apt to fight" (8 [9].1.608b8–11). Point 1 might seem more connected to spirit—but to a strong spirit, which does not fit here. So, Aristotle probably has in mind jealousy for—envy about—the possessions of others, a spouse's affections, and so on. Point 2 is easy to connect to softness: a woman, Aristotle is saying, complains more about pains and discomforts or the absence of pleasures and comforts. As in the first two cases, 3 and 4 must, if Aristotle is consistent, have to do with appetite. The ability to fight well can be connected to spirit; but if Aristotle meant it in that sense, he would have to say women are less apt to fight, not more. Thus, Aristotle is likely saying that just as a woman is more prone to complain about pain and discomfort, she is also more prone to fight with and scold others about them than a man is.

Aristotle also says that women are ἐλεημονέστεϱον: more prone to feel pity, mercy, compassion. This trait is connected to their being more prone to tears—the two are mentioned together at *HA* 8 (9).1.608b8–9— nevertheless, it may be a feeling connected more with spirit than appetite (see *NE* 2.5.1105b21–25, 2.6.1106b18–20). Pity can be felt too much, too little, or the right amount (*NE* 2.5.1105b25, 2.6.1106b19). So Aristotle is saying that in women there is a tendency to feel pity to an inappropriate degree—or, more accurately, to a degree that would be inappropriate for a man. But for a woman, this is fine. In fact, the context from the *HA* 8 (9).1 passage makes clear that Aristotle regards this higher degree of pity or compassion as a positive trait.[20] Perhaps connected to this compas-

---

20. He writes: "This is why a woman is more compassionate than a man and more given to tears, but also more jealous, more complaining, more scolding, and more apt to fight" (608b8–11), thus contrasting a woman's compassion (a positive trait) with her pugnacious side (which is not).

sion is the female's greater concern for the feeding of the young (*HA* 8 [9].1.608b2). But Aristotle provides another reason why, among females of all animal kinds, humans might attend to their children more: "Parents love their children as soon as they are born, while children love their parents only after some time has passed and they have acquired comprehension or perception. From this it is also clear why mothers love their children more [than fathers do]" (*NE* 8.12.1161b24–27). In general, mothers spend more time with their children than fathers do. But it is unclear whether this is a cause of the attention they give their children or the result of the trait mentioned in the *HA* passage.[21]

Here is a final, and very puzzling, character trait: females are more wakeful (ἀγρυπνότερον) than males (*HA* 8 [9].1.608b13). Liddell, Scott, and Jones define ἄγρυπνος as not only "sleepless" and "wakeful" but also "vigilant." This last sense is found in both Plato and Aristotle: Plato says that the guardians of the city must be "wakeful like hounds" (*Republic* 4.404a), and at *Pol.* 5.11, Aristotle says that it is not easy to attack a wakeful (or vigilant) man (1314b35). Being a good guard fits in well with Aristotle's conception of the role the woman should play in the household; but it might seem strange to connect this characteristic to females being softer and less spirited. Being less spirited supposedly makes females less brave and less inclined to act, which does not fit well the image of women as more vigilant. But Aristotle probably shares the view of Xenophon, who says in his *Oeconomica* that "a tendency to be afraid is not at all disadvantageous for guarding things" (7.25, Pomeroy 1994).

Males and females, according to Aristotle, have different character traits—different capacities. As in his biology, where females are presented as physically imperfect compared to males, so too are they presented as "psychologically" imperfect. It may be that Aristotle believed we could not hold it against a woman that, say, she was not as brave as a man. Nevertheless, these differences have two major implications for Aristotle's moral philosophy and his conception of women: (1) the training of the young— for example, girls will have to be watched more closely than boys with respect to sexual activity; and (2) what counts as moral virtue for a man and a woman is different.[22]

---

21. In *GA* 3.2, Aristotle connects a concern for the young in animals with the animal's intelligence (753a5–15).

22. See, esp., *Pol.* 1.13.

CULTURE, CHARACTER, AND GENDER BIAS

Aristotle's conception of the differences between male and female cognitive and character traits fulfills the first requirement of the test for ideological rationalization: his claims do in fact tend to justify the interests of men at the expense of the interests of women. If taken as true—which is how most of them were taken, long before Aristotle, as we'll see—they would tend to justify keeping women inside, keeping a closer watch on women than on men, limiting their social responsibilities, etc.

But what were the sources of Aristotle's views? Were his claims the result of observation and argumentation? And if so, are his arguments so weak as to make us suspect that his conclusions are in general the result of rationalization rather than honest (but mistaken) science?

Let's begin with his remarks about females generally. G. E. R. Lloyd claims that whatever observations were involved—and like Lloyd, I think it's clear that Aristotle did make some astute observations—Aristotle's views about the character of animals and their behavior derive in part from popular belief and folklore, and to that extent they are biased (1983, 18–26). He gives some plausible-enough examples of the influences of folklore (20); nevertheless, nothing Lloyd says in this section—nor in his section on differences between males and females (94–105)—demonstrates that Aristotle's remarks on the differences between male and female character generally (and not specifically between men and women) derive from folklore. Still, he is right that we often cannot tell one way or another what the source of some claim of Aristotle's is. "The female bear and the female leopard or panther . . . are singled out as particularly courageous, though whether this reflects direct or reported observations of their behaviour or stems merely from the popular reputations these creatures had is an open question" (93).

What of Aristotle's views about the character of women in particular? If Aristotle had made observations of the relevant characteristics of the women around him, what would he have discovered? That is, had he looked around the ancient Athenian (or Greek or Mediterranean) world, what might he have concluded about women? It is very likely that, given the social structure(s) of the culture(s) at that time, the women he observed would have been softer and less spirited than men: more docile, less likely to speak out, more controlled than in control. And they may have been more complaining—they had a lot more to complain about—though I see no evidence that they would have been more dishonest and scheming.

But I think Lloyd is right that Aristotle's views on women come, at least in part, "not from literal experience" of the way women are by nature "but from literary or cultural experience" (20). That is to say (and these are my words, not Lloyd's), as part of Aristotle's observations—or data collection—it is very likely that he relied on many of the popular opinions of the times regarding women (some of which are widespread today, e.g., that women are more emotional and prone to tears). For example, in Semonides infamous seventh-century poem, "On Women" (fr. 7, Diehl), women are held to be quite different from men in character, and certain female types are described, many of which (though not all) are similar to the picture that Aristotle presents: women are (or too often are) lazy, complaining, slaves to appetite (being gluttonous and oversexed), dishonest, and plotting. In many other sources, we find women portrayed as deceitful and scheming, ruled by appetites, and cowardly.[23] It is very likely that Aristotle accepted these common opinions. Further, it seems clear that he sometimes applied these common opinions about women to female animals generally. That is the most likely explanation for his claim that "the female is . . . more shameless [than the male], and more lying, readier to deceive" (*HA* 8 [9].1.608b11–12).

Of course, neither Greek tradition nor Aristotle says that all women are slaves to their appetites, mischievous, dishonest, and cowardly. What they report is that women have a greater tendency toward such things, and so men (and society) must act accordingly.

Here is a passage from Xenophon's *Oeconomica* presenting (and defending) much of the "standard" view:

Because both the indoor and the outdoor tasks require work and concern, I think the god, from the very beginning, designed the nature of man for outdoor work. For he prepared man's body and soul to be more capable of enduring cold and heat and traveling and military campaigns, and so he assigned the outdoor work to him. Because the woman was physically less capable of endurance, I think the god has evidently assigned the indoor work to her. And because the god was aware that he had both implanted in the woman and assigned to her the nurture of newborn children, he had measured out to her a greater share of affection for newborn babies than he gave to the man. And because the god had also assigned to the woman the duty of guarding what had been brought into the house, real-

---

23. See, e.g., Hesiod *Work and Days* 42–105, 695–705; Aeschylus *Seven against Thebes* 181–202; Lysius *Eratosthenes* 7–32; and Euripides *Hippolytus* 638–55.

izing that a tendency to be afraid is not at all disadvantageous for guarding things, he measures out a greater portion of fear to the woman than to the man. And knowing that the person responsible for the outdoor work would have to serve as defender against any wrong doer, he measured out to him a greater share of bravery. (7.22–25, revised from Pomeroy 1994)

Aristotle appeals neither to what "the god" has done nor (in the biology) to the division of labor in the household. In his biology, he relies on his observations of (and reports about) nature, including human nature. What he sees is very close to what Xenophon reports: men are better able to endure pain and discomfort than are women; men feel less fear than do women; women love and care for their offspring more than men do. And this was not some idiosyncratic position of two philosophers: it's a fair representation of the ancient Greek way.

Do Aristotle's reliance on the traditional outlook and his observations of everyday life constitute ideological bias? Consider the following case: everywhere a thinker looked, women tended to be (with very rare exceptions) softer and more docile than men, less fierce and less psychologically well-equipped for war, and more attached to their children. One could argue that in such a cultural context, it would not take ideological rationalization to conclude that women are softer and less spirited. We would certainly applaud the intellect capable of thinking in a way more independent of his cultural context and who even devised thought experiments, interviews, and so forth that sought to test his views apart from that context. But at the same time, it would be unfair to chastise a thinker (even a great one) who was unable to free himself entirely from that context—if it was as overwhelmingly uniform as this hypothesis posits. So, was the ancient Mediterranean culture in which Aristotle made his observations so monolithic as to excuse his mistaken conclusions? Or should he have known better?

One way to answer these questions is to raise the issue of exceptions. Were there exceptions to the typical women that Aristotle observed and, if so, was he aware of them? And whether he was or not, could they honestly be regarded as minor exceptions, or should they have led a thinker of Aristotle's caliber to reconsider his position?

As a scientist, Aristotle was aware of the existence of exceptions. Natural phenomena, he says, happen in a given way either always or for the most part (see, e.g., *Physics* 2.8.198b34–199a3; *Metaphysics* 6.2.1026b30–36). Let us focus on male and female bravery, since we actually have some evidence about this. We have seen that Aristotle was aware of exceptions:

"All females are less spirited than males, except the bear and leopard: in these the female is thought to be braver" (*HA* 8 [9].1.608a33–35). It is to Aristotle's credit that he named these exceptions; certainly an ideologically motivated and misogynist biologist would have evaded these "facts" or fudged the results and never have come to such a conclusion.

Was Aristotle aware of particular exceptions among women—for example, women who were braver than men (and not simply because some men were abnormally cowardly)—and if so, did he ignore such exceptions? It is difficult to answer this question with any certainty, but we can speculate. I know of three ancient Greek reports of female bravery in battle: Herodotus mentions Artemisia (probably of Halicarnassus), who fought bravely on the side of the Persians, commanding a ship at the battle of Salamis. Xerxes, Herodotus tells us, said: "My men have become women and my women men" (8.87–88). Later sources also mention a Marpessa (seventh century) and a Telesilla (the fifth century poet), both of whom are supposed to have fought bravely in battle (though both of these stories may be apocryphal).[24] Aristotle makes no mention of any of these, though he must at least have known about Artemisia.

So we do not get too far with exceptions. In the case of animal "bravery," Aristotle was willing to recognize two exceptional kinds of female animals; but in the case of women, he does not mention any exceptions. I believe we have more success in investigating Aristotle on the connection between the physical and the "psychological" and, particularly, his discussion in this connection of the Scythians.

Aristotle believed that there was an intimate connection between body and soul; he rejected the dualism of Pythagoras and Plato. In the opening chapter of his *De anima*, he writes that the affections of the soul (including spirit and appetite) involve the body (403a17; see also *De sensu* 1.439a9). So Aristotle would be inclined to expect that a difference in body would tend to imply a difference in soul—in some respect, though not wholly—and vice versa. And this is often a philosophically sound inference to make. He writes in the *Parts of Animals:*

> Of the instrumental parts that are for defense and protection, nature provides each of them only, or especially, to those animals that are able to use them, and especially to the animals able to use them most—parts such as

24. On Marpessa, see Pausanias 8.48.4–5; on Telesilla, see Pausanias 2.20.8; Plutarch *Moralia* 245c–f; and the *Oxford Classical Dictionary*, 3d ed., s.v. Neither is mentioned by earlier sources.

sting, spur, horns, tusks, and any other such part there may be. And since the male is stronger and more spirited [θυμικώτερον], in some cases he alone has such parts, in other cases he more than the female. For those parts that it is necessary for females to have as well, e.g. parts related to nourishment, they *have*, but they have *less;* while those related to none of the necessities, they do not have. It is also on account of this that among the deer, the males have horns, while the females do not. The horns of female cattle and bulls also differ, and likewise with the sheep as well. And while males have spurs, the majority of females do not. It is the same way too with the other parts of this sort. (3.1.661b28–662a6)

It is not unreasonable to suppose that a male animal with (much larger) horns might be fiercer, say, than a female (of the same kind) that lacks them. Similarly, it makes sense to suppose that a male spider would be much more timid than a female eight times its size (though ultimately, of course, such facts would have to be checked). Aristotle probably reasoned that given that men tended to be larger and stronger than women—and so, for example, better equipped for the battlefield—women were by their nature softer and less spirited than men. Whatever one thinks of this reasoning, it is not gratuitous or arbitrary.[25]

I move now to a narrow instance of Aristotle seeing a connection between the physical and the "psychological," and its relation to our discussion of the source of his views on male and female character. As we saw in chapter 4, Aristotle saw a close connection between females and eunuchs (or eunuch-like men). So, if eunuchs or eunuch-like men tended to be softer and less spirited, this would lend some support to Aristotle's claim that females (who are analogous) might also tend to be by nature softer and less spirited. And he "knew" of such a group of men: certain Scythians. In *NE* 7.7, he writes (in a passage quoted earlier): "It is surprising if someone, with respect to what most are able to withstand, is defeated by them

25. In the biology, Aristotle makes a number of claims based on the connection between the body and the soul, which seem to indicate that he took physiognomy seriously. For example: in *HA* 1.9, he says that rounded foreheads are a sign of spiritedness and straight eyebrows a sign of softness (491b14–15). Similarly, in *PA* 2.4, he sees a connection between the thickness and temperature of blood, and one's spiritedness or timidity (650b27–31); and in *GA* 3.1, discussing the cuckoo bird, he connects cowardice with having a cold temperature (750a11–13). The author(s) of the *Problems* connect(s) temperature and spirit (10.60, 27.3, 30.1). Pseudo-Aristotle *Physiognomics* discusses—among other things—the physical signs of cowardice, softness, effeminacy, and low spirits and their opposites. On this work, and its similarity to Aristotle's own writings, see Lloyd (1983, 19–26).

[pleasures or pains] and is unable to resist them, and not because of hereditary nature or because of disease, e.g., as softness is hereditary among the Scythian kings, and as the female is distinguished from the male [by softness]" (1150b12–16).[26] Aristotle contrasts males and females with respect to softness. He sees a parallel between males and females and between normal males and Scythian kings. This may be significant.

In the Hippocratic treatise *Airs, Waters, Places,* the author describes the Scythians, and much of what he says sounds like a description of eunuchs.

> The Scythian race is as far removed from the rest of mankind as can be imagined and . . . they are all similar to one another. . . . The people differ little in physique as they always eat similar food, wear the same clothes winter and summer, breathe moist thick air, drink water from snow and ice and do no hard work. The body cannot become hardened where there are such small variations in climate; the mind, too, becomes sluggish. For these reasons their bodies are heavy and fleshy, their joints are covered, they are watery and relaxed. . . . All the men are fat and hairless and likewise all the women, and the two sexes resemble one another. . . . They grow up flabby for two reasons. First because they are not wrapped in swaddling clothes . . . nor are they accustomed to horse-riding as children which makes for a good figure. Secondly, they sit about too much. The male children, until they are old enough to ride, spend most of their time sitting in wagons and they walk very little. . . . People of such constitution cannot be prolific. The men lack sexual desire because of the moistness of their constitution and the softness and coldness of their bellies, a condition which least inclines men to intercourse. Moreover, being perpetually worn out with riding they are weak in the sexual act when they do have intercourse. . . . Further, the rich Scythians become impotent and perform women's tasks on an equal footing with them and talk in the same way.

26. Herodotus writes: "Now, on these Scythians who plundered the temple [of Aphrodite Urania] at Ascalon [in Syria] and on their descendents forever the goddess has sent the 'female sickness' [θήλεαν νοῦσον]. As to this, the Scythians say that this is why these people have fallen sick; and they also say that those who come to their country of Scythia can see the condition of those whom the Scythians call 'Enareis'" (1.105; translation from Grene 1987). Later, describing Scythian customs pertaining to divination, he refers to the Enareis as "the men-women [ἀνδρόγυνα]" (4.67). How and Wells write: "The word [Enareis] is probably derived from *a* privative and 'Nar' (Zend., Sansk.), 'a man'" (1928, 1:327).

How and Wells connect (quite rightly, I think) what Herodotus says with the claim of Aristotle: "The disease, described by Herodotus, is said by Aristotle to be hereditary in the Scythian royal families" (1928, 1:107).

Such men are called Anarieis.[27] The Scythians themselves attribute this to divine visitation and hold such men in awe and reverence, because they fear for themselves. . . . They are the most effeminate race of all mankind for the reasons I have given, and because they always wear trousers and spend so much of their time on horseback that they do not handle their private parts, and, through cold and exhaustion, never have even the desire for sexual intercourse. Thus they have no sexual impulses in the period before they lose their virility. (17–22)[28]

If Aristotle could show that eunuchs and eunuch-like men (such as certain Scythians) tended to be softer and less spirited and had physical characteristics like women, he would certainly have some support for the view that there (might) be a connection between being a woman and being softer and less spirited by nature. Aristotle writes: "All animals, when castrated, change over to the female" (GA 5.7.787b19–20), but he never proceeds from this to the claim that eunuchs have female characters. If he simply deduced that eunuchs were softer and less spirited because they physically became like females, that would be an unsupported deduction. But in the case of Scythian kings, Aristotle seems to have found independent evidence that men who are physically like women are also like women in some of their character traits. He reports that they are soft (in the sense described in this chapter), and the author of Airs, Waters, Places reports on their character as well as their bodies: for example, they like to do "women's work."[29]

The big question is, did Aristotle consider the possibility that the ef-

<hr />

27. Compare the Enareis from Herodotus 1.105 and 4.67. See the previous note.

28. Translation from Lloyd 1978.

29. Note that Herodotus, Aristotle, and the author of Airs, Waters, Places are all most likely wrong in at least some aspects of their descriptions of the Scythians (at least the descriptions mentioned in this chapter). Where Herodotus describes a special class of religious seers, Aristotle speaks of kings, and the Hippocratic writer of the rich, and the latter sees this Scythian effeminacy as much more widespread in the population than do Herodotus or Aristotle. Gardiner-Garden writes: "Although Hippokrates' information on Skythian society . . . was probably gathered first hand, the framework within which the material is presented would seem to have been constructed under the influence of a literary tradition" (1987, 36). Similarly, Rolle writes: "Research and a number of newly discovered accounts of the Scythians have in the meantime confirmed that we are dealing here [i.e., in the Hippocratic account] with an extremely biased account, saturated with personal aversions, which was at best only accurate when describing exceptions" (1989, 55). (In general, see Rolle, chap. 4.) On the tendency of the ancient Greeks to view non-Greek—and especially Eastern—kings as effeminate, see Gambato (2000).

feminate Scythians were the way they were not owing to nature but because of how they lived? The author of *Airs, Waters, Places* certainly made such a connection—in fact, he argues that they are the way they are because of their climate and clothing and too much horseback riding. Aristotle may very well have known of this description of the Scythians, but he makes no mention of the connection the author of *Airs, Waters, Places* makes. But should he have?

Aristotle often connects locality with an animal's characteristics. For example, pigs from mountainous and rough terrain are wilder and fiercer than other pigs (*HA* 7 [8].29.607a9–13). But in an important passage in *GA* 4.6, Aristotle does a bit more than assert such a connection. He writes that most women (in comparison to females of other kinds) suffer discomfort in connection with gestation.

> Now the cause of this is to some extent attributable to their manner of life, which is sedentary, and this means that they are full of residue; they have more of it than the other animals. *This is borne out by the case of those tribes where the women live a life of hard work. With such women gestation is not so obvious, and they find delivery an easy business. And so do women everywhere who are used to hard work.* The reason is that the effort of working uses up the residues, whereas sedentary women have a great deal of such matter in their bodies owing to the cessation of menses during gestation, and they find the pains of delivery severe. Hard work, on the other hand, gives breath exercise, so that they can hold it; and it is this which determines whether delivery is easy or difficult. (775a31–b2, emphasis added)

In general, Aristotle believes that different locations will in part determine different characteristics.[30] But in *GA* 4.6, he makes it clear that it is not simply locality but lifestyle as well that determine these general characteristics. This counts against Aristotle's science here: Why is it, we may ask, that the characteristics of women in Athens or in Greece are to be taken as the characteristics of women by nature? Why didn't Aristotle conclude merely that Greek women are less spirited and softer than Greek men? If he wished to argue that the way Greek women are is in fact better (or even more natural), he could try to do that on other grounds. But he does not. He seems simply to take the Greek social structure as what is natural. Even if he thought that Athens or Greece generally was culturally superior to her neighbors—and I would agree with him here—it is the fallacy of division

---

30. See Aristotle's discussion of the spirit of Europeans, Asians, and Greeks at *Pol.* 7.7.1327b23–1328a7.

(and more) to argue that Greek culture is superior (more consistent with our natures as human beings, say) to every other culture, therefore, how women live in Greece is in every respect superior to how they live in every other culture—and, in fact, is natural and good.

Lloyd notes that Aristotle's observations about the characteristics of animals "range from the frankly fabulous to the acutely observed" and concludes: "A considerable body of ideas that have their origins in popular belief and in folklore thus finds a place in Aristotle's zoological investigations" (1983, 20, 24). It is true that some of Aristotle's claims about male and female cognitive and character traits come from popular belief—which by itself does not constitute an ideological influence, on my view. Still, there is evidence that Aristotle could have raised doubts or questions about some of his claims but did not because of his assumptions about the general correctness of Greek culture. On many of the issues covered in this chapter, Aristotle's concern for the opinions of the many and the wise may have caused him to hesitate—or reject the need—to ask such questions. To the extent that he failed to explore these issues fully, his description—with its numerous derivative claims and implications—of females as softer and less spirited than males is strongly tainted by ideological presuppositions, despite being based, in many ways, on observation and various degrees of plausible reasoning.

| # ARISTOTLE ON FEMALES:
AN ASSESSMENT OF THE BIOLOGY

My aim has been to investigate what Aristotle said in his biology about females, what arguments and/or observations led him to say what he said, and
finally, whether there is any evidence that what he said was the result of ideological rationalization. Let me summarize the results of this investigation.

FEMALES IN ARISTOTLE'S BIOLOGY: A SUMMARY

Aristotle writes about several physical differences between males and females, many of which point to the physical inferiority of females, as he sees
it. Some of these claims are accurate; many are not. Females, he claims,
tend to be, in comparison to males, weaker, less muscular, shorter, slim-
mer, and slighter (though for some kinds of insects, females are larger).
They have softer flesh, paler skin, smoother feet, thinner shins, and softer
bones than males do. Women are unable to go bald, though they have less
hair on their bodies. Females lack, or possess smaller, defensive parts (e.g.,
horns), and the females of some kinds (including women) have fewer teeth.
Females are cooler (their blood is not as warm as the blood of males), and
as a result, they have smaller brains and fewer sutures in their skulls.

According to Aristotle, males and females both contribute something
to generation, but their contributions are different. Females contribute
menses, which is seed, but not fully concocted seed (though the female is
capable of some concoction). The female's contribution constitutes all of
the matter for generation. The female seed is shaped primarily by the contribution from the male and, thus, becomes an embryo and eventually a
fully formed animal. The female seed is passive in the sense that, in generation, the male seed does the forming, while the female seed is what is

formed; but it is not passive in the sense of being inert or indeterminate matter. Finally, the female contribution is in part responsible not only for the number and size of offspring but also for an offspring's possession of a nutritive soul and its gender and appearance.

Aristotle's remarks in the biology about female character are consistent with what he says elsewhere, and his overall conception of a woman's moral character reads like a list of history's clichés about them: women are—again, in comparison with men—tamer, more delicate, and more sensitive and yet Hell hath no fury like a woman scorned; they are more impetuous and emotional but also much less capable of withstanding pain and discomfort; they tend to be less brave (except for female bears and leopards); they tend to be scheming, dishonest, and bitchy; and yet they also, by nature, make the best parents; and so on. Just as Aristotle regards females as generally physically inferior to males, so he sees them as "psychologically" inferior: they are softer and less spirited—that is, the female is weaker than the male when it comes to her spirit and her soul's control over her appetites.

REASON OR RATIONALIZATION

How could Aristotle have come to hold such a conception of the female? Is the picture he paints, though generally erroneous, the result of reason—of honest, objective science? Or is it the result of ideological rationalization? This question has been answered in the preceding chapters.

It is true that Aristotle got some things right in his biology about females: in some insects, females are larger than males; females and males both contribute something significant to generation (and not an incubator and homunculus, respectively); women are similar to eunuchs in a number of interesting ways; females tend to lack or have smaller defensive parts; and obviously, females are (or tend to be) physically different from males in many ways other than in respect to genitalia, for example, in height, size, shape, strength, voice.[1] But there are also errors. For example: the gender of the different types of bees; the details of what males and females each contribute to generation (and the actual process of generation generally); some purported physical differences between males and females, for

---

1. This very brief sketch of one narrow issue—the nature of females—does not do justice to the magnificent breadth of what Aristotle accomplished in his biology. See Balme (1987, 16–17) and the passage from Ogle (1882), quoted in chap. 5, app. A, above.

example, that females have fewer sutures in their skulls and fewer teeth; the claim that female lions are not predators; and so on.

As we have seen, not all of Aristotle's mistakes were unavoidable and/or based on the limitations of the state of science at the time he worked. In my investigation of his claims about females in the biology, I did occasionally catch a (sometimes faint) whiff of ideological influence or motivation. I found some possible and/or partial traces of bias in the claim that females have paler skin; the insufficient research into the number of teeth; the occasional quickness with which Aristotle applies to some cases the generalization that males are physically superior to females; the fact that the connection he makes between soft flesh and intelligence is not applied to females; and finally, much of what he says about the character of females. In all of these cases, I found the possibility (and, occasionally, the probability) of some kind of ideological influence or motivation. Nevertheless, these traces of bias are not overwhelming or primary or fundamental.

Aristotle was a scientist and a philosopher. As we have seen—especially in his discussion of generation—his biology is framed or presented in a philosophical context; it relies to a large degree on certain philosophical presuppositions. That having been said, as illustrated throughout this book, Aristotle's views about women and other females, however mistaken, were largely the result of empirical science—of reasoning based on observation—not of misogyny and ideological rationalization. With some exceptions, Aristotle went as far as he could go with the available evidence (including the nature of the cultures he observed) and given his lack of, say, a microscope. Ideology was not a major source of his views. Basically, he was an honest and objective scientist who sometimes had a difficult time escaping his cultural context and who, in some cases, was sloppy in his investigations, perhaps because of ideological factors. But the idea that his remarks about females were primarily the result of ideological presuppositions and rationalizations—or even worse, misogyny—is without foundation. For the most part, Aristotle's discussions in the biology of females pass the ideology test described in chapter 1.

ARISTOTLE AND HIS FEMINIST CRITICS

The same cannot be said of the statements of many of Aristotle's harshest critics. Cynthia Freeland, an excellent commentator on Aristotle but often too generous to some of his more careless feminist critics, writes: "Feminists seem not to have looked beyond what Aristotle actually says about females in his biology to examine what he implies (as Irigaray would put it) in his metaphors, syntax, grammar, and his silences" (1994, 151). But the problem is not that some feminists have failed to look beyond what Aristotle actually says; rather, they have failed to look at what he says. The knee-jerk reactions—the automatic accusations of misogyny—whenever such critics encounter Aristotle's remarks about king bees, fewer teeth in women, and (if they bother to read it) the complex discussion of the female contribution to generation, suggest a biased, fundamentally ideological motivation on their part, not a "passionate search for passionless truth" (as John Herman Randall described Aristotle's intellectual life).[2]

Martha Nussbaum wrote that in his biology, Aristotle sometimes "said stupid things without looking" (1998, 250). I disagree. But even if it were true, how much worse are those commentators of Aristotle who—over two thousand years after Aristotle—say stupid things without looking (or, more accurately, without reading)? Even if Aristotle were guilty of some rationalization, it would not approach the degree of ideological bias at work in many of the feminist critics who accuse him of bias. We have seen a few examples already, especially in chapter 3. Another is Ruth Bleier, who in her *Science and Gender: A Critique of Biology and Its Theories on Women,* writes: "It was not limits of observation that misled earlier centuries of scientists concerning the facts of generation; rather it was the 20-centuries-long concept, stemming from Aristotle, that women, as totally passive beings, contribute nothing but an incubator-womb to the developing fetus that springs full-blown, so to speak, from the head of the sperm. One's conceptual framework, a certain state of mind, permits one to see and accommodate certain things but not others" (1984, 3). Clearly, only a "conceptual framework" or "state of mind" hostile to Aristotle could have enabled Bleier—and a host of other scholars—"to see and accommodate certain things but not others" and, thereby, to conclude that Aristotle's so-called misogyny was the source of much of what he says in his biology.

What Bleier says about Aristotle—and particularly the details of his account of generation—is clearly false. But such a warped picture of Aristotle supports her agenda—bashing the "patriarch" behind the (very "pa-

2. Randall 1960, 1. I am not complaining that all feminists regard Aristotle as a misogynist, though certainly many do. Actually, it is now a trend among feminist Aristotle scholars to see Aristotle, whatever his errors, as a source for—as quite compatible with—feminist thought. For example, this is the general tenor of the essays in Freeland (1998a). (One section of Freeland's introduction is titled "Feminists Recover Aristotle.") I cannot here discuss the plausibility of this trend.

triarchic") history of biology?—whereas the truth does not. Her account of Aristotle fails the ideology test.

ARISTOTELIAN SCIENCE AND ARISTOTLE'S
REMARKS ABOUT FEMALES

Discussing Aristotle's teleology, Allan Gotthelf writes that Aristotle "does not attempt to legislate a priori the particular form which a successful account of the natures and potentials of living organisms must take. . . . There is nothing in the fundamentals of Aristotle's philosophy, and nothing in his philosophical and scientific method, which would prohibit the adoption of [another] thesis, should the scientific evidence be judged to warrant it" (1987a, 229).

Aristotle came to conclusions about living things in the context of his philosophy (and his culture). But this does not change the fact that he had confidence in, and was motivated by, the ability of reason based on the evidence of the senses to discover truths about the natural world. For the most part, what he concluded about females was based on the strength of the evidence available to him. At times, he may not have pursued an issue vigorously enough because of ideological assumptions, but generally, his observations of the world were central to his biology.

It has been said that Aristotle would have changed his cosmology had he had access to Galileo's telescope.[3] Similarly, he would have changed much of what he thought about embryology if he had had a microscope. And he would have changed his mind about the capabilities of women (e.g., concerning their ability to be scientists or philosophers) after one conversation with a female scientist or philosopher—though not with some of his harshest feminist critics, whom he might easily have taken as evidence for his original position.

3. See Randall 1960, 161–62.

Ankney, C. D. 1992. "Sex Differences in Relative Brain Size: The Mismeasurement of Woman, Too?" *Intelligence*, vol. 16.

Asso, Doreen. 1983. *The Real Menstrual Cycle*. Chichester: John Wiley & Sons.

Balme, David, trans. [1972] 1992. *Aristotle's De partibus animalium I and De generatione I (with passages from II 1–3)*. Rev. ed. With a Report on Recent Work and an Additional Bibliography by Allan Gotthelf. Oxford: Clarendon Press.

———. 1985. "Aristotle *Historia Animalium* Book X." In *Aristoteles: Werk und Wirkung*, edited by J. Wiesner. Vol. 1. Berlin: Walter de Gruyter.

———. 1987. "Aristotle's Biology Was Not Essentialist." In Gotthelf and Lennox 1987.

———. 1990. "Matter in the Definition: A Reply to G. E. R. Lloyd." In *Biologie, logique et métaphysique chez Aristote*, edited by Daniel Devereux and Pierre Pellegrin. Paris: Éditions du CNRS.

———, ed. and trans. 1991. *Aristotle: History of Animals*. Vol. 3, *Books VII–X*. Loeb Classical Library. Cambridge, Mass.: Harvard University Press.

Barnes, Jonathan. 1984a. "Aristotle on Women." Review of *Science, Folklore and Ideology*, by G. E. R. Lloyd. *London Review of Books* (February 16–29).

———, ed. 1984b. *The Complete Works of Aristotle: The Revised Oxford Translation*. 2 vols. Princeton, N.J.: Princeton University Press.

Beavis, Ian C. 1988. *Insects and Other Invertebrates in Classical Antiquity*. Exeter: University of Exeter Press.

Bleier, Ruth. 1984. *Science and Gender: A Critique of Biology and Its Theories on Women*. New York: Pergamon.

Blum, Deborah. 1998. *Sex on the Brain: The Biological Differences between Men and Women*. New York: Penguin-Putnam.

Blundell, Sue. 1995. *Women in Ancient Greece*. Cambridge, Mass.: Harvard University Press.

Bolton, Robert. 1987. "Definition and Scientific Method in Aristotle's *Posterior Analytics* and *Generation of Animals*." In Gotthelf and Lennox 1987.

Braybrooke, David. 1967. "Ideology." In *Encyclopedia of Philosophy*, edited by Paul Edwards. Vol. 4. New York: Macmillan Publishing and the Free Press.

Brothwell, Don, and Patricia Brothwell. 1969. *Food in Antiquity: A Survey of the Diet of Early Peoples.* London: Thames & Hudson.

Byl, Simon. 1975. *Recherches sur les grands traités biologiques d'Aristote: sources écrites et préjugés.* Brussels: Royal Academy.

Cavarero, Adriana. 1995. *In Spite of Plato: A Feminist Reading of Ancient Philosophy.* New York: Routledge.

Charlton, William. [1970] 1992. *Aristotle's Physics I–II.* Rev. ed. With a Note on Recent Work. Oxford: Clarendon Press.

Claeys, Matthew C., and Sharon B. Rogers. 2003. "Sheep Facts." *Animal Science Facts,* March 24 (www.cals.ncsu.edu/an_sci/extension/animal/4hyouth/sheep/sheepfacts.htm).

Coles, Andrew. 1995. "Biomedical Models of Reproduction in the Fifth Century B.C. and Aristotle's *Generation of Animals.*" *Phronesis* 40, no. 1.

Cooper, John. 1990. "Metaphysics in Aristotle's Embryology." In *Biologie, logique et métaphysique chez Aristote,* edited by Daniel Devereux and Pierre Pellegrin. Paris: Éditions du CNRS.

Currie, Sarah. 1989. "The Bellies of Women and the Minds of Men: Women and Food in Ancient Society." In "Food, Health and Culture in Classical Antiquity," edited by Peter Garnsey. Working Papers no. 1. Cambridge University, Department of Classics.

Davies, Malcolm, and Jeyaraney Kathirithamby. 1986. *Greek Insects.* Oxford: Oxford University Press.

Dean-Jones, Lesley Ann. 1994. *Women's Bodies in Classical Greek Science.* Oxford: Clarendon Press.

Dorfman, Ralph I., and Reginald A. Shipley. 1956. *Androgens: Biochemistry, Physiology, and Clinical Significance.* New York: John Wiley & Sons, Inc.

Dover, K. J. 1989. *Greek Homosexuality.* Updated and with a new postscript. Cambridge, Mass.: Harvard University Press.

duBois, Page. 1988. *Sowing the Body: Psychoanalysis and Ancient Representations of Women.* Chicago: University of Chicago Press.

Düring, Ingemar. 1943. *Aristotle's "De partibus animalium": Critical and Literary Commentaries.* Göteborg: Elanders Boktryckeri Aktiebolag.

Elshtain, Jean Bethke. 1981. *Public Man, Private Woman.* Princeton, N.J.: University of Princeton Press.

Feyerabend, Paul. 1970. "Consultations for the Specialist." In *Criticism and the Growth of Knowledge,* edited by I. Lakatos and A. Musgrave. Cambridge: Cambridge University Press.

———. 1975. *Against Method.* London: New Left Books.

———. 1987. *Farewell to Reason.* London: Verso.

Fias Co. Farm. 1997–2003. "How to Estimate a Goat's Age." *Goat Health and Husbandry* (http://fiascofarm.com/goats/age.htm).

Flashar, Hellmut. 1962. *Aristoteles: Werke in deutscher Übersetzung.* Band 19, *Problemata Physica.* Berlin: Akademie Verlag.

Fortenbaugh, W. W., et al. 1992. *Theophrastus of Eresus: Sources for His Life, Writings, Thought and Influence.* 2 vols. Leiden: E. J. Brill.

Freeland, Cynthia. 1992. "Aristotle on the Sense of Touch" In *Essays on Aristotle's De Anima,* edited by Martha C. Nussbaum and Amélie Oksenberg Rorty. Oxford: Oxford University Press.

———. 1994. "Nourishing Speculation: A Feminist Reading of Aristotelian Science." In *Engendering Origins: Critical Feminist Readings in Plato and Aristotle,* edited by Bat-Ami Bar On. Albany: State University of New York Press.

———, ed. 1998a. *Feminist Interpretations of Aristotle.* University Park: Pennsylvania University Press.

———. 1998b. "On Irigary on Aristotle." In Freeland 1998a.

Furth, Montgomery. 1988. *Substance, Form and Psyche: An Aristotelian Metaphysics.* Cambridge: Cambridge University Press.

Gallop, David. 1996. *Aristotle on Sleep and Dreams.* Warminster: Aris & Phillips.

Gambato, Maria. 2000. "The Female-Kings: Some Aspects of the Representation of Eastern Kings in the *Deipnosophistae.*" In *Athenaeus and His World: Reading Greek Culture in the Roman Empire,* edited by David Brand and John Wilkins. Exeter: University of Exeter Press.

Gardiner-Garden, John R. 1987. *Herodotos' Contemporaries on Skythian Geography and Ethnography.* Papers on Inner Asia, no. 10. Bloomington: Indiana University, Research Institute for Inner Asia Studies.

Garnsey, Peter. 1988. *Famine and Food Supply in the Graeco-Roman World: Responses to Risk and Crisis.* Cambridge: Cambridge University Press.

———. 1989a. "Food Consumption in Antiquity: Towards a Quantitative Account." In "Food, Health and Culture in Classical Antiquity," edited by Peter Garnsey. Working Papers no. 1. Cambridge University, Department of Classics.

———. 1989b. "Infant Health and Upbringing in Antiquity." In "Food, Health and Culture in Classical Antiquity," edited by Peter Garnsey. Working Papers no. 1. Cambridge University, Department of Classics.

———. 1989c. "Malnutrition in the Ancient World *or* Was Classical Antiquity a Third World?" In "Food, Health and Culture in Classical Antiquity," edited by Peter Garnsey. Working Papers no. 1. Cambridge University, Department of Classics.

———. 1999. *Food and Society in Classical Antiquity.* Cambridge: Cambridge University Press.

Gibbons, Ann. 1991. "The Brain as 'Sexual Organ.'" *Science,* vol. 253.

Gotthelf, Allan. 1985. "Notes towards a Study of Substance and Essence in Aristotle's *Parts of Animals* ii–iv." In *Aristotle on Nature and Living Things: Philosophical and Historical Studies Presented to David M. Balme on His Seventieth Birthday,* edited by Allan Gotthelf. Pittsburgh: Mathesis.

———. 1987a. "Aristotle's Conception of Final Causality." In Gotthelf and Lennox 1987.

———. 1987b. "First Principles in Aristotle's *Parts of Animals.*" In Gotthelf and Lennox 1987.

Gotthelf, Allan, and James Lennox, eds. 1987. *Philosophical Issues in Aristotle's Biology.* Cambridge: Cambridge University Press.

Grene, David. 1987. *The History of Herodotus.* Chicago: University of Chicago Press.

Grote, George. 1883. *Aristotle.* 3d ed. London: J. Murray.

Harig, Georg, and Jutta Kollesch. 1977. "Neue Tendenzen in der Forschung zur Geschichte der Antiken Medizin und Wissenschaft." *Philologus*, vol. 121.

Hogan, James. 1984. *A Commentary on the Complete Greek Tragedies: Aeschylus.* Chicago: University of Chicago Press.

Horowitz, Maryanne Cline. 1976. "Aristotle and Women." *Journal of the History of Biology*, vol. 9.

How, W. W., and J. Wells. 1928. *A Commentary on Herodotus.* Oxford: Clarendon Press.

Hudson-Williams, T. 1935. "King-Bees and Queen-Bees." *Classical Review*, vol. 49.

Huby, Pamela. 1985. "Theophrastus in the Aristotelian Corpus, with Particular Reference to Biological Problems." In *Aristotle on Nature and Living Things: Philosophical and Historical Studies Presented to David M. Balme on His Seventieth Birthday*, edited by Allan Gotthelf. Pittsburgh: Mathesis.

Irigaray, Luce. 1993. "A Chance for Life: Limits to the Concept of the Neuter and the Universal in Science and Other Disciplines." In *Sexes and Genealogies*. Translated by Gillian C. Gill. New York: Columbia University Press.

———. 1998. "Place, Interval: A Reading of Aristotle, *Physics* IV." In Freeland 1998a.

Isselbacher, Kurt et al. 1980. *Harrison's Principle's of Internal Medicine.* 9th ed. Tokyo: McGraw-Hill.

Jaeger, Werner. 1948. *Aristotle: Fundamentals of the History of His Development.* Translated by Richard Robinson. Oxford: Oxford University Press.

Jones, Horace Leonard. 1929. *The Geography of Strabo.* 8 vols. Loeb Classical Library. Cambridge, Mass.: Harvard University Press.

Kahn, Charles. 1990. "Comments on M. Scholfield." In *Aristoteles Politik: Acten des XI. Symposium Aristotelicum, Friedrichshafen/Bodensee 25.8–3.9.1987*, edited by Gunther Patzig. Göttingen: Vandenhoeck & Ruprecht.

Keuls, Eva. 1993. *The Reign of the Phallus: Sexual Politics in Ancient Athens.* 2d ed. Berkeley: University of California Press.

Lange, Lynda. 1983. "Woman Is Not a Rational Animal: On Aristotle's Biology of Reproduction." In *Discovering Realities: Feminist Perspectives on Epistemology, Metaphysics, Methodology, and Philosophy of Science*, edited by Sandra Harding and Merrill B. Hintikka. Dordrecht: D. Reidel.

Lebeck, Anne. 1988. "The Commos in the *Libation Bearers.*" In *Aeschylus's "The Oresteia,"* edited by Harold Bloom. New York: Chelsea House Publishers.

Lennox, James. 1981. "The Anti-Philosophy of Science." *Objectivist Forum* 1 (June).

———. 1985. "Demarcating Ancient Science: A Discussion of G. E. R. Lloyd, *Science, Folklore and Ideology.*" *Oxford Studies in Ancient Philosophy*, vol. 3.

———. 1996. "Aristotle's Biological Development: The Balme Hypothesis." In *Aristotle's Philosophical Development: Problems and Prospects*, edited by William Wians. Lanham, Md.: Rowman & Littlefield.

———. 1999a. "Aristotle on the Biological Roots of Virtue: The Natural History of Natural Virtue." In *Biology and the Foundation of Ethics*, edited by Jane Maienschein and Michael Ruse. Cambridge: Cambridge University Press.

———. 1999b. "The Place of Mankind in Aristotle's Zoology." *Philosophical Topics*, vol. 27.

———. 2001a. *Aristotle: On the Parts of Animals I–IV.* Oxford: Clarendon Press.

———. 2001b. *Aristotle's Philosophy of Biology: Studies in the Origins of Life Science.* Cambridge: Cambridge University Press.

Lewes, G. H. 1864. *Aristotle: A Chapter from the History of Science.* London: Smith, Elder.

Lloyd, G. E. R. 1966. *Polarity and Analogy: Two Types of Argumentation in Early Greek Thought.* Cambridge: Cambridge University Press.

———, ed. 1978. *Hippocratic Writings.* London: Penguin Classics.

———. 1979. *Magic, Reason and Experience.* Cambridge: Cambridge University Press.

———. 1983. *Science, Folklore and Ideology: Studies in the Life Sciences in Ancient Greece.* Cambridge: Cambridge University Press.

Mayhew, Robert. 1997a. *Aristophanes: Assembly of Women.* Amherst, N.Y.: Prometheus Books.

———. 1997b. *Aristotle's Criticism of Plato's "Republic."* Lanham, Md.: Rowman & Littlefield.

Nussbaum, Martha. 1982. "Saving Aristotle's Appearances." In *Language and Logos: Studies in Ancient Greek Philosophy Presented to G. E. L. Owen,* edited by Malcolm Schofield and Martha Craven Nussbaum. Cambridge: Cambridge University Press.

———. 1985. *Aristotle's "De motu animalium."* Princeton, N.J.: Princeton University Press.

———. 1998. "Aristotle, Feminism, and Needs for Functioning." In Freeland 1998a.

Nye, Andrea. 1990. *Words of Power: A Feminist Reading of the History of Logic.* New York: Routledge.

Ogle, William. 1882. *Aristotle on the Parts of Animals.* London: Kegan Paul, Trench & Co.

Peck, A. L. 1942. *Aristotle: Generation of Animals.* Loeb Classical Library. Cambridge, Mass.: Harvard University Press.

Pomeroy, Sarah. 1994. *Xenophon Oeconomicus: A Social and Historical Commentary.* Oxford: Clarendon Press.

Provet. 1999–2002. "The Dental Formula for Humans and Different Domesticated Species." *Provet Information for Animal Health* (www.provet.co.uk/health/diagnostics/dentalformulae.htm).

Rand, Ayn. 1988. "The Psychology of Psychologizing." In *The Voice of Reason: Essays in Objectivist Thought.* Edited by Leonard Peikoff. New York: New American Library.

Randall, John Herman. 1960. *Aristotle.* New York: Columbia University Press.

Richardson, John T. E. 1997. "Introduction to the Study of Gender Differences in Cognition." In *Gender Differences in Human Cognition,* edited by John T. E. Richardson. Oxford: Oxford University Press.

Rolle, Renate. 1989. *The World of the Scythians.* Translated by Gayna Walls. London: B. T. Batsford Ltd.

Ross, David. 1955. *Aristotle Parva Naturalia.* Oxford: Clarendon Press.

Rosser, Sue. 1992. *Biology and Feminism: A Dynamic Interaction.* New York: Twayne Publishers.

Russell, Bertrand. 1950. "An Outline of Intellectual Rubbish." In *Unpopular Essays.* London: George Allen & Unwin Ltd.

Sass, Louis. 1992. *Madness and Modernism.* Cambridge, Mass.: Harvard University Press.

Schofield, Malcolm. 1990. "Ideology and Philosophy in Aristotle's Theory of Slavery." In *Aristoteles Politik: Acten des XI. Symposium Aristotelicum, Friedrichshafen/Bodensee 25.8–3.9.1987,* edited by Gunther Patzig. Göttingen: Vandenhoeck & Ruprecht.

Segal, Charles. 2001. *Oedipus Tyrannus: Tragic Heroism and the Limits of Knowledge.* 2d ed. Oxford: Oxford University Press.

Sokal, Alan, and Jean Bricmont. 1998. *Fashionable Nonsense: Postmodern Intellectuals' Abuse of Science.* New York: Picador.

Sommerstein, Alan. 1989. *Aeschylus: Eumenides.* Cambridge: Cambridge University Press.

Sprague, Rosamond Kent. 1985. "Aristotle on Red Mirrors (*On Dreams* II 459b24–460a23)." *Phronesis,* vol. 30, no. 3.

Thomson, D'Arcy Wentworth. 1910. *The Works of Aristotle Translated into English.* Vol. 4, *Historia Animalium.* Oxford: Clarendon Press.

Tuana, Nancy. 1994. "Aristotle and the Politics of Reproduction." In *Engendering Origins: Critical Feminist Readings in Plato and Aristotle,* edited by Bat-Ami Bar On. Albany: State University of New York Press.

Ussher, R. G. 1973. *Aristophanes Ecclesiazusae.* Oxford: Oxford University Press.

van der Eijk, Philip J. 1999. "*On Sterility* ('*HA* X'), a Medical Work by Aristotle?" *Classical Quarterly,* vol. 49, no. 2.

Zeitlin, Froma. 1988. "The Dynamics of Misogyny: Myth and Mythmaking in the *Oresteia.*" In *Aeschylus's "The Oresteia,"* edited by Harold Bloom. New York: Chelsea House Publishers.

INDEX LOCORUM

INDEX OF NAMES

This index is limited to modern figures. For other names, see the general index and index locorum.

DATE DUE

GAYLORD	No. 2333		PRINTED IN U.S.A.